SCALE UP

YOUR PROFITS

Special <u>FREE</u> Bonus Gift for You!
To help you earn more revenue in your business,
I am offering a FREE Bonus.
Go to **www.RoyceTalks.com**
And request a resource guide on
Press Releases

ALL RIGHTS RESERVED. No part of this book or its associated ancillary materials may be reproduced or transmitted in any form or by any means, electronic or mechanical, including photocopying, recording, or any informational storage systems without permission from the publisher.

Disclaimer and/or legal notices. While all attempts have been made to verify information provided in this book and its ancillary materials, neither the author or publisher assumes any responsibility for errors, inaccuracies, or omissions and is not responsible for any financial loss by customer in any manner. This book is not intended for use as a source of legal or financial advice. If advice in these areas is needed, the services of a qualified professional should be sought.

Published by: RoyceTalks, LLC

Printed in the United States

Copyright © 2019 RoyceTalks

ISBN: 9781688130265

What Others Say About Royce and Her Marketing Expertise

"Good evening. I showed the sales letter to the attorney and you received rave reviews. Thank you again."--Donnell B, consumer product inventor

"Wow! I'm speechless! No words to describe your work. Thank you. I would love to work with you again. Your words inspire people; I'm not kidding."--Wayne B, cosmetic company founder

"These blogs are awesome! It's like you are a magician! I'm just so amazed...."--Sherri E, Hospitality Recruiter

"I want to thank you for your amazing work. The blog received a lot of views today after I posted it. I referred you to my friend who publishes a magazine. He was so impressed with your writing."--Mauricio H, Staffing Agency

"I love what you wrote! I'm glad I asked you to write my content."--Tracy F, Personal Organizer

"I really want to dominate Google and I love your content!"--Karl F, Realtor

"I highly recommend Royce as a marketing consultant. I have seen the impact of marketing strategies she has designed and implemented for companies and non-profit organizations that helped them overcome existing challenges, identify new opportunities, and position them to thrive in a dynamic market place. She's passionate about helping businesses identify their unique strengths, build their customer base, and establish brand loyalty. Royce will help you kick your business into high gear."--Sylvia J, Realtor

"Royce is an excellent writer and researcher. She's thorough, detail oriented and innovative. Royce delivers high quality copy in a timely manner. A good communicator, Royce is a pleasure to work with."--Bree Goldstein, Professor of Internet Marketing, UCF

"Good evening. I showed the sales letter to the attorney and you received rave reviews. Thank you again." --Donell Branch, Inventor of Accuracy Ball

"Wow! I'm speechless! No words to describe your work. Thank you. I would love to work with you again. Your words inspire people; I'm not kidding." -- Andy Koo, Munmo Cosmetics

"Thanks so much for the articles. I love them all. Very well written and exactly what I'm looking for." — Delia, Raw Beauty Minerals

"These blogs are awesome! It's like you are a magician! I'm just so amazed...." -- Sherri Elmore, CEO, Southern Hospitality Search

"I want to thank you for your amazing work. The blog received a lot of views today after I posted it. I referred you to my friend who publishes a magazine. He was so impressed with your writing." -- Mauricio Henderson, Recruiter and CEO, Perseverance Staffing

"I love how this blog is written, awesome work!! I would like to continue working together, I will be planning a few campaigns and blog ideas for this year and will keep you updated." — Carina, La Moda Lingerie

"I love what you wrote! I'm glad I asked you to write my content." -- Personal Organizer

"I really want to dominate Google and I love your content!" -- Karl Freund, Broker, Kenneth James Realty

"Royce Gomez definitely has a way with words. I listed her home and she offered to write the listing description. She did an amazing job touching on all the key informational pieces that make a buyer want to look at, and be excited about a home. Her home got some great interest and was under contract in 48 hours. Realtors that want some extra flare in their listing descriptions and need quality content to position themselves as an expert in their targeted field would greatly benefit from her expertise and her training." —Caroline Ritterling, Keller Williams Agent

"Just went through all the emails and I am very happy with the wording and tone of them. I have no doubt that my customers will respond positively to them. I will definitely be in touch soon with more work." —Demi, Lagos Garden Centre

#Share

To order large quantities of this book for your

Employees or association, fill out the contact form at:
www.RoyceTalks.com

Royce Gomez may be the ideal speaker for your next event!

Any organization, association, or corporation who wants to provide knowledge to help their team generate more revenue may want to consider inviting Royce for a keynote or workshop training.

To book Royce to speak:
www.RoyceTalks.com
719-684-4676

TABLE OF CONTENTS

Secret #1...These SEO Elements Need Your Attention Now

Secret #2...Tips for a Successful Email Marketing Campaign

Secret #3...How to Get the Best Results from Your Facebook Ads

Secret #4...Steps to Creating a Successful Blog for Your Business

Secret #5...Is Your Website an Effective Sales Funnel?

Secret #6...How to Write an About Us Page for Your Website

Secret #7...Why Simple is Better in Web Design

Secret #8...How to Rebrand Your Business

Secret #9...The Elements of Your Social Media Strategy You Can't Ignore

Secret #10...Optimizing Your Website for Mobile Users

Secret #11...Outdated SEO Practices You're Probably Still Using

Secret #12...What to Do About a Negative Search Result for Your Company

Secret #13...Repairing the Damage of Bad Online Reviews

Secret #14...How to Use Instagram for B2B Marketing

Secret #15...How to Make Your Instagram Page Stand Out to Customers

Secret #16...Habits of Successful Social Media Influencers

Secret #17...7 Things You Should Never Post on Your Business Facebook Page

Secret #18...How to Conduct an SEO Audit For Your Website

Secret #19...Reasons Your Website Doesn't Rank on Google

Secret #20...Social Media Cliches You Shouldn't Use in Your Marketing

Secret #21....6 Tools to Aid Your SEO Campaign

Secret #22...How to Write a Better Blog Post

Secret #23...What to Know About Google SEO Updates of 2017

Secret #24...Beginner Graphic Design Tools Anyone Can Use

Secret #25...How To Market Yourself As A Freelancer Online

Secret #26...Social Media Schedulers You Can Use for Free

Secret #27...How to Set Up a Content Calendar

Acknowledgements

#1
These SEO Elements Need Your Attention Now

Search engine optimization is the forefront of online marketing strategy everywhere. Over 80% of consumers use search engines as a research tool before making a purchase. This means whether you're generating leads online or in-store, your customers want to have a relationship with your brand through a website or through social media.

Your brand's online presence is one of your most important assets. Like any other marketing campaign, you need to maintain, adjust, and track your SEO progress, which is time sensitive. SEO strategy is ever-changing, so you need to keep a watchful eye on the trends. With every new year comes a new set of rules and best practices for search engine marketing.

The goal of any SEO campaign is to attract customers who search for your products, services, or brand online. When a customer searches for keywords (search terms that describe the content on a web page or website) related to your brand, you want your website to be at the top of the search engine results page (SERP). Which websites "rank" or appear at the top of the SERPs is determined by the search engine itself, such as Google or Bing. The search engines use different algorithms to determine this based on what content is the highest quality and most related to the user's keywords.

Though the search engine algorithms are not public knowledge, marketers study trends and watch for indicators of higher or lower ranking in the system. Most SEO tactics focus on improving the quality and customer experience of the site, choosing keywords that target customers are likely to use, and creating content around those words. There is no one right way to do this. It requires trial and error and testing on the marketer's part. However, over the years we've discovered the basic factors that contribute the most to SEO success.

These factors matter to every website, no matter the size of your brand or target market. For your site to succeed, these are the areas that you need to improve now:

Mobile optimization

It's important to know where your customers are spending the most time, and how to reach them with your marketing content. On average, consumers spend 69% of their personal media time on their smartphone, rather than a desktop, and this trend will continue to rise. Customers want to engage with social media and look up local businesses on-the-go. Your first online interaction with a customer is very likely to be on their smartphone, so it's important to make that first impression a good one.

Unfortunately, brands spend the majority of their time working on the technical and content marketing components of their SEO campaign, and ignore mobile optimization. Many websites do not function fully in their mobile versions, making it difficult for customers to get the information they need to make a purchase or contact the business. Making your website mobile-friendly only takes a few simple steps, and it will improve your conversion rates and lead generation results tremendously.

Accommodating to changes in Google algorithms.

Over 80% of online searches begin on Google.com. The most effective way to strategize your SEO campaign is to follow Google's best practices, as most other search engines will follow suit. Google regularly updates its algorithms to better the user experience. They can determine a website's context, its theme, and its desktop and mobile usability through the use of site "crawlers," or bots that sweep your sitemap looking for keywords and other useful information.

Google often changes their ranking criteria, and you need to know about these changes to improve your strategy. Do proper research, as many SEO tactics used even just last year may be ineffectual. You don't want to be penalized or lose ranking for poor, outdated SEO practices.

Topical targeting.

Search engines now rank sites based on their variety, rather than similarity of keywords. Instead of using the same few keywords for each page, they encourage sites to use a choice of many different keywords that surround a topic or theme. This is to improve the user experience, so that sites are built for the benefit of the customer rather than optimized for the search engine alone.

This is to discourage the practice of "keyword stuffing" where sites overuse the same keywords on every page in an attempt to increase their ranking. This used to be an effective practice, when search engine crawlers gathered very basic information, without any context. Now, search engines can interpret the context of a site as well as how reader-friendly it is. This advancement is called the "semantic search" capability, and your site can be penalized for keyword stuffing or using other practices meant to benefit the search engine rather than the user.

Progress on your offsite SEO.

Most of your campaign will be focused on the technical aspects and content creation for your site, or the "on-site" best practices of SEO. However, these are not the only factors that the search engines factor in to choose their highest ranking sites. "Off-site" SEO is the cultivation of positive endorsements and links back to your brand from other places online.

"Backlinking" is considered one of the most important aspects that search engines use to rank their sites. The more links that refer to your site, the more trustworthy your content is deemed by Google. You can build a strong off-site strategy by guest blogging for other brands, getting endorsements, and listing your site on online directories.

These SEO elements are vital to the success of your marketing campaign and your business' online reputation. While most of these can be improved upon by your team, it never hurts to talk to an SEO professional about ways in which you can bring your site to the top of the SERPs.

#2
Tips for a Successful Email Marketing Campaign

You business needs to invest in email marketing today if you haven't already. Think it's a waste of time? These statistics will make you think again:

- Email marketing has an ROI of 3800%
- On average, you get $44 back for every $1 spent on email marketing campaigns
- The value of an email marketing campaign is at least three times higher than that of any social media

Email marketing is the pivotal point of digital marketing where you can convert leads and nurture your existing customer relationships. While SEO, social marketing and digital advertising can generate leads, most of these practices cannot convert nearly as effectively as email marketing. This is because you have a narrowed audience, one which has expressed interest in your brand and opted in to your marketing messaging. No other online customer segment is as willing and ready to buy as your list of email subscribers and you should take advantage of that.

Any company can start a successful email marketing campaign without a tremendous budget. With the right tools to compose, segment and track your campaigns, you can see incredible results. There are a few basic rules you should follow, but luckily the more simplistic you make your emails, the more likely they are to generate qualified leads. Unlike SEO and social media, email marketing is something that doesn't need to be active daily. You want your customers to be informed and target your messages towards their individual needs and buying behavior.

To make your email marketing campaign a real success, here's what you need to remember:

Make it valuable to subscribe, and easy to unsubscribe.

Getting subscribers to your list is the most difficult step. The consumer, even if they are interested in your company, does not want to be bombarded by spam emails and promotions. They will be hesitant to sign up for a newsletter unless you have established trust and offer something of value to them in exchange for their information.

Websites accomplish this in a number of different ways. Some require users to give their emails in order to view certain types of content or offer gifts to reward users who sign up. In order for this to work, you need to determine what your customers want and need the most. If you have a high-quality blog on your website, an exclusive e-book or promise of unreleased content, this may interest your users. If you're trying to sell products directly on your site or through email, you may consider offering a discount or free item when users sign up.

Because email marketing is more personal, and more intrusive than other forms of online marketing, you also need to make sure customers can opt out at any time. Just because a customer unsubscribes from your list doesn't mean they weren't positively influenced by your email marketing. However, if you make it a hassle for them to do so, you may turn a satisfied customer into an angry one. Never send follow-up emails after a user unsubscribes, unless they are still a paying customer.

Send a welcome email.

Immediately after a user subscribes, this will be the most likely time for them to engage. Your company is fresh on their minds, and they may even be considering a purchase. Grab their attention immediately with a welcome email that thanks them for their interest and offers a reward for their subscription, such as a discount or valuable content they couldn't get on your website.

Your welcome email should be short and conversational. Use images to communicate as much as text so that your welcome seems inviting. You can feature top-selling products or link popular blog posts to redirect users back to your site once more. Most importantly, your email should be tailored for the individual customer. Use their name, and reference products or content they may have clicked on during their site visit. This will establish trust with the customer, and make them more likely to open your next email.

Don't send unless you have something to say.

The reason most people will unsubscribe from an email list is because they begin to expect "noise" rather than quality, informative content. Unless you are having a sale, new product release, or other pertinent consumer information to share, an email update is unnecessary. If your customers expect noise, they'll ignore it. But, if every email they receive has beneficial information for them, they'll keep reading.

Test different emails and track your results.

You'll need to work on different ways of translating your brand voice into email format. This isn't as easy as it sounds because email formats don't typically allow for a great deal of text. Like with social media, you'll be limited on the amount that you can say before losing the interest of the reader. Plus, most consumers view emails on smartphones as much or more than they do on desktop, so you need to find templates that convert well to mobile applications.

A/B testing different email texts, images, formats, and segmentation is essential to finding the right style for your newsletters. Get creative, and try different approaches to see what customers respond best to. There's no right or wrong way, just the way that works best with your audience.

Now that you know the best practices to make your email marketing campaigns work, it's time to start writing.

#3

How to Get the Best Results from Your Facebook Ads

Marketers love Facebook, the largest social platform ever created, and the one that permanently transformed digital media for individuals and businesses alike. Facebook is the digital marketer's most important tool for consumer engagement. You use it to manage your business' online presence, connect with potential customers, and communicate with existing ones.

Facebook advertising is the most weighted aspect of your social media marketing strategy as a whole. Organic reach is important, but without paid advertising your brand may be overshadowed. Facebook advertising is not the place to cut costs in your marketing budget, and here's why:

- *Facebook ads are easy.* Once you set up your page, Facebook will walk you through the steps of creating your ad. As you create more ads, you'll learn what performs best. Plus, the application lets you know your approximate reach from the beginning of the campaign, and allows you to track your progress in real time.

- *Facebook ads are highly customizable.* Unlike other online platforms, Facebook allows you to control the majority of your ad features, functions, and creative components. Your ad must follow basic guidelines and fit within the Facebook format; but, you can control your audience, the ad creative and ad objective to ensure you get the best results for your work. They consistently add new features to the Business Manager so you can explore new tactics and options with every new campaign.

- ***Facebook ads are effective.*** Facebook has over 1 billion users, all of whom willingly opt in to advertising from local businesses on the network. The platform allows you to see information about every user who follows or engages with your page, giving you valuable information about your most active audience.

Facebook ads are highly effective, but not for the reason you may think. They are not made for customers to find you, but rather for *you* to find your best customers. Many marketers become discouraged when their ads don't sell, but they are missing the point. Every interaction a consumer has with your brand is tracked. You may not make the sale on Facebook; but, you are gaining all the information you need to target that customer offline and convert the lead.

That being said, Facebook ads can be effective for online sales. Your industry and general success with online sales will determine if your products are likely to sell on social media. For example, the apparel industry has a very low Cost-Per-Action (the average amount spent to get a customer to engage or opt-in to an ad), as opposed to finance and tech.

Facebook ads are the most effective online ads you can run for your company. Even search engine advertisements aren't as effective as those run on social platforms, and Facebook's advertising options are by far the most business-friendly and cost-effective. But, how do you know your ads will be able to compete with all the others on the network?

If you want to make the most out of your Facebook ad budget and time, these are the four rules you need to follow.

Track your audience.

As mentioned, the greatest benefit of Facebook advertising is the data you can collect about your customers. Facebook ads will let you track which customer segments are most active, when they're most likely to engage, and what types of posts perform the best on your page, both organic and paid. Tailoring your ads to these demographic and behavioral markers is essential for social marketing success.

Get quality images.

Facebook ads allow for very little text. The part that will stand out to your audience as they scroll down their feed is the images and videos you choose to include in your ad creative. Choose photos that are branded, colorful, and easy to understand even without the headings and text. Stock images will work, but it's best to work with a graphic designer or photographer to get unique, quality images that are all about your brand. This is especially important if you are trying to sell a product directly from the ad.

Try different forms of copy and content.

No two Facebook ads have to be the same. There are hundreds of options within Facebook's guidelines, and adding your own custom images and text make the possibilities even greater. Experiment with different tones, length of copy, and types of visual content to see what performs best. Perhaps your video ads receive more engagements, but blog shares lead to more sales. You can compare these results in your Business Manager app, and adjust your campaign accordingly.

Always keep them fresh.

It's important to schedule ads regularly, or you may unfortunately experience a drop in your organic results. Don't run the same ad for too long, or you may get repeat views and tire your audience Instead, try to schedule a different ad every week, with a consistent budget so you can accurately compare results and improve.

With the right strategies in place, there is no reason why your business can't succeed in Facebook advertising.

#4
Steps to Creating a Successful Blog for Your Business

In the modern world, an incredible amount of information is available to us online. There's a website dedicated to almost any topic you can think of, and an expert on any niche field you want to learn. As a business, it's your job to become the expert, to own the website people go to when they're looking for answers. But, you face thousands of competitors who also want to grab the attention of your target market.

Where do consumers go for the information they're looking for? Comprehensive websites, like WikiHow and Ask.com, are popular for short, simple answers, but when a consumer is looking for all the facts, they often go to a professional website for the authority opinion. You, as a business owner, are the authority they're looking to find. In order to have the opportunity to market to these consumers, you have to educate through informative blog content.

A blog is a website, or page of a website used to share information and opinions about a specific subject. Personal and business blogs are traditionally written in "post" format, where short bits of information are shared in a page-long article. Business blogs are used to help attract consumers who are searching for answers to their questions, and to inform customers about products, services, and company news. Blogs increase your online visibility, and provide a platform to engage with your consumers.

The harsh reality is that most blogs, no matter how informative the content, go unnoticed. It takes a lot of work to keep a blog fresh and create new posts to attract customers. However, the only way to make a blog successful is to start writing content and follow a strategy that increases its visibility. You can't use a blog for SEO and social marketing until you have one, so here are the steps to creating and posting quality content your users will love:

Step 1: Choose your domain.

If you're starting from scratch, you need to secure a domain immediately. Choosing a domain that customers will remember is an important part of your branding. Different blogging platforms may allow you to create a site with a free domain, but it is preferable to have one of your own.

If you already have a company website, you can add a page to it dedicated to your blog content. Most web builders will have a template for blog pages to make this step easier. You want your blog page to be incorporated on your site, unless you use a platform such as Medium or Wordpress for SEO purposes.

Step 2: Choose your web hosting.

Choosing the right hosting service makes a tremendous difference in the quality of your blog. Use a platform that is user friendly, and not too hard to customize. When choosing a hosting service or web builder, look for the following attributes:

- Visually appealing templates
- User-friendly administrative functions
- Strong site security
- 24 hour support

There is nothing more frustrating than trying to make changes to your blog and not being able to figure it out yourself, or running into a problem with no support team to contact. Shop for different packages and find the one that's best for your needs.

Step 3: Optimize your site's blog template.

Once you've chosen your hosting service, you can start creating posts. However, before you publish, you'll want to make sure that the template you choose is both user-friendly and SEO compatible. With most blogging platforms, you can customize your posts to match the look and feel of your website. You'll also want to view the tagging options, and see what portions of the blog's display (such as the meta description, title, images, etc.) you can change.

Using the same template for all of your blog posts creates continuity for the reader. It also eases the burden on you when it comes time to start writing and posting.

Step 4: Choose topics you want to cover.

Your blog should contain information pertinent to your customers and company. For SEO purposes, you want to choose niche topics that answer your customers' most important questions. For content ideas, look at your competitors' blogs. What topics do they spend the most time covering? And what can you do differently to outshine them?

Step 5: Create a monthly content plan.

For a blog to be effective, it needs to be consistent. Posting on a daily or weekly basis is the only way to get your content to rank well in the search engines, and gives repeat visitors something new to read every time. You need to have a content plan at least a month in advance so you can schedule posts and ensure your blog never goes out-of-date.

Final Step: Start writing!

Now that you've created your blog and planned posts to engage your audience, it's time for you or your professional writer to start blogging. To add momentum to your campaign, start sharing your work on social media. The sooner you start, the better your blog will become.

#5

Is Your Website an Effective Sales Funnel?

Any marketing campaign can be understood through the concept of the sales funnel. A sales funnel is a marketing tool or set of objectives that leads a customer towards the decision to buy. Several actions must be taken by the customer to move from one stage of the sales funnel to the next. This concept is used to better target consumers at different stages in the funnel, and to improve assets that lead them to take desired actions. The stages of the sales funnel are:

- *Awareness Stage* - A customer has his or her first encounter with the brand or product.

- *Interest Stage* - The customer identifies a need that the product or service can satisfy, and develops an interest in the possible benefits.

- *Consideration Stage* - The customer does research, comparing the product to other solutions provided by competitors.

- *Decision Stage* - The customer has determined one product is the best solution for their needs, and prepares to purchase or negotiate with the company.

- *Buying Stage* - The final transaction takes place.

- *Evaluation Stage* - The customer uses the product or experiences the service, and makes a judgment on the quality received. They may leave feedback, discontinue use, or consider more products and upgrades from the original purchase.

- *Re-purchasing Stage* - This is when the cycle starts again; the customer becomes aware of a new product or additional service by the company, and considers their next purchase.

For any type of e-commerce company, the website alone must move the customer through each of these stages. The customer may contact a representative or visit the store, but the bulk of the work rests in the effectiveness of the website to reach certain objectives and continue the momentum of the sales process. This is a significant challenge, as online sales are impersonal and there is not a salesperson to help answer customer questions.

Does your website effectively take the customer from awareness to purchase? To make your website an effective sales funnel from beginning to end, ask yourself the following questions:

Is your SEO campaign driving traffic?

80% of consumers start from a search engine to make purchases or research products. For your customer to become aware of a new product and reach the consideration stage, they have to be exposed to your website first. The goal of your SEO campaign is to drive traffic to your site, so that it can effectively do its job in providing information and buying options to consumers. Check your Google Analytics to see how many new visitors are reaching your site, and how many of your web pages are ranking for page one on your targeted keywords.

Is your landing page effective?

Once customers reach your site, are they welcomed and directed to the pages they need? The only way for them to begin the consideration stage is to be presented with the most important information upfront. Over half of users will spend less than 15 seconds on your site; the best way to get them to explore is to create a visually appealing, informative landing page.

Do you present front-end offers well?

The customer is trying to make the decision between choosing you and a competitor when they visit your website. In order for them to make the right decision, they need as much information as possible, from multiple sources on your website. When you list products on your site, include a detailed description, past customer reviews, and FAQs. This information serves as the replacement for your salesman in an online format.

Do you have a back-end upsell?

Once the customer makes a purchase, you want them to do two things: 1) leave a positive review, and 2) buy from your site again. The way to make these two things happen is in the upsell, after the purchase is finalized. Follow up with them, asking for their feedback, and include information about supplementary products or products related to their search queries.

Can you engage with customers from the site even if they don't buy?

Not every visitor to your site is ready to buy. However, every visitor should become a lead, regardless of where they are in the sales funnel process. If they didn't make a purchase, did they click on an item? Can you gain their contact information to follow up later? Your website needs to be effective in gathering contact information, as well as demographic data so you can better target and market to that user in the future.

Your website can be a comprehensive tool for lead generation and sales if you design strategically and incorporate effective SEO practices. The quality of information you present to the customer is crucial. Your online presence may be the only impression of your company that the customer receives. That first impression could lead to a final sale when you follow best practices.

The best way to create a lead-generating website is to be informative, up-to-date, and user-friendly. The details don't matter as long as you make the journey through the sales funnel easy for the user to follow.

#6

How to Write an About Us Page for Your Website

Creating the perfect website for your business isn't just marketing. It's an art. The designs, the content, and the social aspects of your website come together to give your users an amazing brand experience from the comforts of home. It's the gateway to your company culture. It's the invitation to customers to learn about you and everything your company can do.

A good website is an art form. A poor website is just a collection of words and buttons that don't mean anything to the consumer. The elements you choose and the content you create make the difference. A balance of good content and web design is essential. You want your users to be impressed by the design, informed by your content, and able to navigate your website easily.

One of the most important pages on your site, even more important than your product pages, is the "About Us" section. This page of your website tells the customer who you are, and why they *need* to choose you over the competition. This is where your brand gets the chance to shine!

Elements of an About Us Page

- An introduction of your company
- Staff introductions or bios
- The company "story"
- A Call-to-Action
- Contact information

Your About Us page should not only tell the customer who you are, but why your company is different. It should also prompt the customer in some way to take the next step, whether that is making a purchase, subscribing to your newsletter, or following you on social media. There is no one right way to create your About Us page, yet there are ways in which you can make yours stand out.

Include photos and video.

Every page of your website should include alternative media, not just text. But your About page should feature many different visual elements that tell the story of your brand. You can include infographics, photos of the staff, promotional videos, and much more. Visual elements not only give a lot of information to consumers, they elicit an emotional response that helps your customers connect to the brand.

Share your Company Philosophy.

A mission statement is standard on an About Page; don't make yours generic. You want to give consumers a reason to connect with your brand. They want to know what you stand for, why your company is important, and how their purchase can improve their lives or someone else's. If your company donates or partners with a charity, tell your users about it. Studies show that brands who advocate for social and environmental causes are more successful with millennial audiences because the customer's purchase has meaning behind it.

Tell your story, don't just tell the facts.

Many company About pages only tell the facts of the business, but not the story behind it. Your customers want to know about the entrepreneurs who started your company. It makes your brand relatable, more of a person and less like a corporate entity. Your About Us page can be from the perspective of the business owner or president, as long as you incorporate their story with the story of the company itself.

Write in a way your customers will understand.

Corporate jargon and excessive keywords are not meant to be on your About page. This is the platform to be personable, to talk about the people who make your company what it is. You don't have to use a strictly professional tone. Write your About Us page as if you were talking directly to the customer, not as a salesperson, but as a fan of your own brand. You want to convey value and establish trust. To do that, talk to the customer in a language they understand.

Gain their trust.

When customers read your About Us page, you need to show your true personality and gain their trust to buy from you. Now that online shopping is the way to go for most people, it is harder to build customer loyalty. You don't have salespeople for the customer to connect to and ask questions, so your About page needs to serve that purpose.

FAQs.

A "Frequently Asked Questions" section, if not a separate page itself, can be included on your About page (or as a subpage). This is a great platform to communicate to your customers about your products, and give them all the information they need to buy. Oftentimes, if a customer is unsure about a product's features, they will simply choose a different solution rather than ask you questions. Making it easy for them makes it easier for you to make the sale.

Your About page can become the center of attention for your website, if written and designed well. Include these elements and nothing will be lacking for your customers when they reach it. Remember, the best About pages are unique. They establish trust and show the customer what your brand and team can do for them.

#7
Why Simple is Better in Web Design

"It's the simple things in life that are the most extraordinary."

More blogs, more product pages, more CTAs… the ongoing trend in digital marketing is *more, more, more*. But, to stand out you want to do something different. The customer doesn't benefit from bigger, more complex web design. While larger sites can rank better in the search engines, your visitors will appreciate a site that is short, sweet, and succinct.

Don't shy away from simple, bold web designs. Studies have shown that simplistic websites often have lower bounce rates, and rank just as well in the search engines as large, complex sites. Focusing your content on a few core pages, and minimizing the "clutter" will not only help your customers have a better user experience, but it can help you turn leads into sales better than a bigger website can.

How Simple Websites Are Better for Users

Simple designs load faster for users. This is true for both mobile and desktop applications. A faster load speed is a significant advantage in terms of SEO. The faster your website appears, the less likely it is for a customer to "bounce," or leave your site after only viewing one page. Lower bounce rates, as well as the load speed itself, are factors that Google accounts for in its rankings on the search engine results pages. Plus, your users will have an easier time finding information, and an overall better experience.

A simple design may seem less "marketing friendly," but it is more customer friendly. Most of the content on a website is there for the marketer's advantage - for better rankings, more keywords, and seemingly more opportunities to communicate your brand message. However, most customers only view two or three pages of your site - at best - to find what they need. The more cluttered and wordy your site becomes, the harder it is for the user to find the content they want.

Having a simpler site also makes it easier for you to guide customers in to taking certain actions. If your customers have to go through two or three landing pages to get to the product or content they want, they may abandon the search and look for another site. If you want to shorten the customer buying journey, take them directly to the content you want them to see. You don't need many landing pages and popups to convince a user to make a purchase they may already be poised to make.

Simple websites don't feel or look spammy so they establish trust more quickly with customers. No one wants to feel like they're being pressured or aggressively marketed to. A simple design will allow the user to feel that they are in control. The less you give them, the more they will want to learn on their own.

The Psychology Behind Simplicity

To understand how web design works, and what elements make some designs most effective, we need to look into how the brain processes information and stores it in memory. All marketing is based on psychology and how we can apply these concepts to guide consumers to purchase. Your website design is an important part of this process. With the overload of information people receive online day to day, you need to make your website stand out in the minds of your users.

One of the most basic psychological elements of web design is "cognitive fluency". Cognitive fluency, by definition, describes how easy it is for someone to think about and understand a concept. So, the easier it is for someone to understand the layout of your website, the better their experience will be.

For example, have you ever seen a website where the Home button was at the bottom of the front page? Of course not! It's always at the top. Users expect to know where the Home button is on every web page, whether they've visited it before or not, because *that's how things are supposed to be*. Basic designs, like the web templates that you would use on Wordpress or Squarespace are based on this principle. This isn't to stifle creativity, but rather to help marketers create websites that are easiest for users to understand.

The second psychological reason simple web designs are effective has to do with your memory. Your "working memory," or the part of your memory that stores immediate information, can only hold a certain amount at a time. The less visual information you have to process, the easier it is for you to remember that information. A large website, with page upon page for a user to sift through, will give users plenty of content, but they won't remember most of it. If you simplify your website to a few core elements, users may not learn as much, but they will remember it.

A Great Example of Simple Yet Powerful Web Design

Visit Seth's Blog. This website, created by one of the greatest marketing minds, is a great example of how a simple website can carry a powerful message. It only has one page, the blog feed, and a sidebar for useful links and his email subscription. It doesn't get much simpler than that, and Seth's Blog is one of the most popular blogs online today. Users can get all the content they need without having to leave the main page. It's visually appealing, easy to understand, and immensely popular for a reason.

To create the best website for your brand, you don't have to go overboard. Give your users exactly what they need. You don't need to impress with a monster website. If you get the basics down, you'll have a stellar website that speaks for itself.

#8

How to Rebrand Your Business

Branding is arguably the most important aspect of your business. More so than the products, or your ratings, reviews, and publicity. A brand makes your company. Even the highest quality product on the market is nothing without a solid brand behind it. It encompasses who you are as well as what you do. It defines your business to the audience and is the medium in which you communicate with them.

Branding is essential, which is why it can be so hard to master. Every element of your business, from the team members you choose to the label you put on the box, is the brand. If it doesn't resonate with customers, your product simply won't sell. So, what happens if you get your branding wrong?

Many companies start out with an idea of what they want their company image to be. But, if what the entrepreneur sees doesn't align with what the customer sees, you have a problem. The right product used with the wrong brand voice can turn a stellar idea into a huge flop. That's why it is important not only to create a solid brand, but to accept feedback and change when your company needs it.

- **Brand voice** - *The expression and communication of a brand through words, prose, and content that motivates consumers to buy.*

Creating a brand voice is a lot more than writing about your company, products, and services. It's the way you relate to your consumers, and how they perceive your brand on an individual level. The nuances of your brand's communication style play an important role in how you win a customer's loyalty and repeat purchases.

Your brand voice has to change as your company does. As you expand to new markets, or as your audience changes its views based on cultural influence, you too have to change. Some brands can successfully modernize or redefine their brand image, but many others make mistakes that cost them the loyalty and trust of their customers.

Here is how you can avoid those mistakes and stay in touch with your audience:

Redefining your target market.

If you're making a change in your target market (perhaps to reach a younger audience or to expand your reach to a niche demographic), you need to study your market and understand what speaks to them. You cannot make assumptions on how a particular audience will perceive your marketing efforts. Instead, you must ask, learn, and eventually experiment with different communication tactics that prove effective.

When branching out into new territory, you have to ask, "How will this new segment of customers improve my business?" You have to decide whether they are worth the rebranding effort, and if so, how much of your core business are you willing to change to meet their expectations.

Sometimes a business just needs a "fresher" look, whether that be in signage, media assets, or logo design. These elements are easy to change and can improve customer perceptions across the board.

Start slow.

If you want to make a dramatic change in brand identity, you have to do so in small steps. Otherwise you will alienate your existing customers, and likely lose their trust very quickly. What would you think if you were used to a brand's light-hearted sense of humor and fun, and suddenly they take on a very structured corporate communication style? Would it make sense to you? And would you want to continue doing business with a brand that's inconsistent?

If you decide to make a change, do so gradually. It's important that you don't alienate existing customers while trying to attract new ones.

Reverse engineering.

It's never a bad idea to take cues from highly successful competitors in your niche. Take a look at different brands, both in your industry and outside, to see what communication styles are used for different audience demographics. When you see what works for others, use it in your own marketing messaging. You don't want your brand voice to sound generic; however, you also don't want to go completely against the grain of what your customers are used to from brands like yours. Researching your competitors can also help you generate ideas for marketing campaigns, content, and more.

Test reactions with your existing customers.

Sometimes a change in brand voice does not go over well with your existing audience. While you may want to make a bold shift, some forms of humor, brand values, and other communication do not go over well with all demographics. If you do decide to go in a bold, new direction, do so in incremental steps, and see if there is a change in engagement. Ask for direct feedback from your customers as well.

Brand voice is the most influential part of your company image. If you don't get it right, you could lose potential business. But, if you have a plan in place, and continually tailor your brand to the needs of your consumers, you'll receive unique brand loyalty that's impossible to replace.

#9
The Elements of Your Social Media Strategy You Can't Ignore

Social media is the rule not the exception anymore for successful marketing campaigns. Every business is online, and whether you're active or not active on social channels, you send a message to consumers about your brand. Some companies see social media as just another platform for advertising, but there is so much more that you can do with the right plan in place.

The goals of a social media strategy are different for every business. If you're an online retailer or e-commerce business, you may want to use the platform to generate leads or even sell directly. However, if your business is service-based, you may use your social profiles as a way to reach out to customers to receive feedback and testimonials for your company.

What You Can Accomplish Through Social Media:

- Gain reviews for your company
- Perform customer support functions and improve customer experience
- Test ad creative and brand messaging
- Share content from your website and gain traffic
- Improve SEO rankings
- Sell products and services directly
- Network with potential clients and partners
- Communicate quickly and effectively during a company crisis
- Connect with influencers to promote your brand

You must remember that social media is a two-way street. Unlike other forms of marketing, you are not in control of everything said about your brand, or who can interact with your profiles versus who cannot. Because of this, you need to use social media as a comprehensive business tool, not just a marketing platform.

You should focus on these three areas of your social media strategy to gain the most benefit for your business:

1. Customer Service.

Consumers don't typically use social media for online shopping, but they do use it to communicate and share their experiences with brands. They also want to be able to reach a business if they have questions or concerns. Quality customer service, therefore, should be your top priority when using social media for your business.

When a customer reaches out on social media, make sure to respond promptly. If a review (positive or negative) shows up on your page, be sure to address it with sincerity and either thank the customer for their support or ensure their complaint is resolved, not just acknowledged. Customer reviews play a crucial role in online sales, and that includes your reviews on social media. The more positive press you can get from customers on your pages, the better.

2. Research.

Social media analytics are one of the most powerful tools for marketers. They're updated instantly so you can track your progress and measure customer demographics and engagement on a daily, weekly, or monthly basis. No other tool is more efficient in tracking your audiences' buying behaviors. When you run ads on social media, you get an even better picture of customer preferences, interests, and opinions of your brand.

Social media gives you a clear and comprehensive picture of your audience, so use it to strategize your other marketing efforts. Social media gives you an unbiased view of your customer segments so you can write better content, target the right consumers, and use this data rather than paying for it through another medium (or worse-- guessing). Using the analytic tools, you can target your digital ads based upon your stats on social.

3. Content.

Content is the backbone of your brand voice online. Creating consistent and engaging content not only gives your followers a chance to learn more about you; but, it can boost your SEO efforts and relevance in the community. Blog posts and videos are very popular on social sites. They are the most shared types of content online, and what you should use most on your social profiles. However, you have to choose content carefully before posting.

Informative articles and posts about your brand may be useful, but they won't engage all audiences the way interactive content (such as videos, events, and interactive posts) do. Make your social pages about your brand culture and identity, rather than just a platform for selling online. You should use humor if it fits with your brand. Most people use social networking sites to relax and have fun, so if your brand can provide that, it will attract followers.

The most important thing to remember is that social media isn't just a marketing tool. It's an overall experience of your brand for consumers, and should be taken advantage of for more than just advertising. There is so much that social media has to offer, for both your company and customers, and endless ways in which you can add value to your brand simply by using these platforms.

When you focus on these three elements of your social campaign, your marketing efforts will start to flourish. Great customer service, compelling content and a marketing plan based on relevant data are more valuable than anything else in your marketing strategy.

#10

Optimizing Your Website for Mobile Users

Search engine optimization for marketers is about to go through major changes, and we all need to be prepared. In 2016, Google released a statement on the updates for their mobile indexing systems. The new algorithm used for ranking sites is a "mobile-first system." In their statement, they announced that, "Our algorithms will eventually primarily use the mobile version of a site's content to rank pages from that site."

This is a very positive advancement for consumers. Over 60% of the searches are conducted on mobile devices, with even higher numbers for certain industries and categories. Users live in a mobile-friendly world, and it's our job to ensure they get the best experience.

In light of the "Possum" update, Google and AnswerLab conducted a 119-hour long research study to determine what makes mobile websites most user-friendly. To help marketers prepare for the update, they compiled a list of best practices for web designers to follow.

There are three core elements that Google urges site developers to focus on: speed, display, and local optimization. While the update won't change the ranking factors involved in site indexing, these elements are often changed when mobile versions of sites are used. To make sure your business doesn't slow down after the Possum update, follow these guidelines for mobile optimization and configuration:

Site Speed

Site speed is an important ranking factor for both mobile and desktop; however, greater emphasis is put on site speed in a mobile-first system. Your hosting service plays an important part in how fast your site will load, as well as the user's device. But, there are design elements you can alter to increase load speed, regardless of your hosting service.

- Images tend to take up much of your mobile site's loading time. You can reduce the image file size in a mobile version, as less detail is necessary for a smaller screen.
- You also want to minimize code written for your site. Unnecessary, redundant or complex code can be harder for the browser to load.
- Reduce redirects from your site. A redirect URL is one that takes users and search engine crawlers to a primary URL used for the site. This slows down loading time, and can hurt your rankings.

Design

Most businesses don't bother using a mobile version of their site, but they should. Desktop versions are not translated best to mobile, unless the developer uses a responsive design. A responsive design will translate your site to mobile automatically; however, you can use a separate version of your site for mobile with most web hosting services.

There are advantages and disadvantages to both. Responsive designs require less work upfront, however they cannot account for every nuance of mobile usage, and tend to fall short of Google's best practices. A separate mobile version allows you to tailor your user experience for mobile search, however this requires additional time and investment. Depending on your industry (restaurants and retail usually have more mobile traffic) and current mobile capabilities, you may consider using a separate mobile version for your content.

Regardless of whether you use a responsive design or separate mobile URL, there are minor changes in your mobile design that will improve the user experience tremendously:

- Reduce popups and buttons where users may accidentally click
- Resize text and images so they are easy to see on mobile screens
- Align touch elements so they are not too close together, making it more difficult for the user to navigate the site.
- Use your descriptions and titles pointedly to reduce the amount of text. Include keywords in your headers and meta descriptions while keeping your content clear and concise.

Local optimization

Another Google research study showed that, "50 percent of consumers who conducted a local search on their smartphone visited a store within a day." If you have a physical store location or target demographic area, local optimization is not an option. You should include content with the name of your city and state. Use your location in your headers, tags, body text, and urls.

Can I Use an App for Mobile?

Because mobile usage is now more prevalent than desktop search, many companies are switching to apps to improve the customer experience. The question is can an app replace the mobile version of your site?

The simple answer is yes you can use an app, but you need a mobile website too. The interstitial page (essentially a popup) that is used to redirect users from the search engine to the app may block Google's crawlers. This can cause problems for indexing and may lower your rankings. Interstitial usage can also cause poor user experiences, which Google is trying to avoid with their new update.

Making your site mobile friendly will improve your customer relationships and your relationship with the search engines. Now is the time to change and put your business on the mobile map.

#11

Outdated SEO Practices You're Probably Still Using

Search engine optimization is a full time job for your marketing team. With every year Google releases new updates to their system as they move towards better user experiences and search results. These updates keep marketers at the top of their game. Consistent research is necessary to make sure your website follows current SEO protocol.

But, there isn't a guidebook for us to use and make sure we're doing the right things. Google provides as much information as they can to marketers, although we never know exactly what the algorithms are looking for and how our sites measure up. This is why many third-party research teams study the SERPs, looking for changes in ranking to determine which sites perform best and what other sites need to do to change.

This research helps marketers update their strategies for best results. Yet, there is always something more we can do to ensure our websites are at peak performance. You may not realize it, but your SEO playbook could be out-of-date and causing problems in your progress that you're completely unaware of.

Many of these practices were once in use, but now are ineffectual at best and cause for penalization at worst. You want to avoid these SEO tactics because they waste your time and energy and can hurt your website rankings permanently. The best thing to do now is to run an audit on your website, looking for indicators of these common mistakes:

Using the same keywords over and over.

When SEO was first developed as a marketing strategy, search engine crawlers were very simple. They simply looked for the user's search terms on top-ranking websites. Volume of keywords was essential to ranking. Because of this, it was effective to use as many of the same or similar keywords on each page, oftentimes sacrificing the quality of content for better rankings.

They now have a name for this, "keyword stuffing", and not only is this ineffective, it can actually cause your site to be penalized. Keyword stuffing lowers the quality of content for the user, tricking the search engine into thinking a site is more relevant to a user than it actually is. That is why Google released the "Penguin" update, eliminating the problems caused by this black-hat SEO trick.

After Google's Penguin update, crawlers now use "semantic search," in website ranking. This means they can detect the subject and direct users to relevant sites based on keywords that are similar. You don't have to use every keyword variation for Google to understand your content. Excessive use of keywords is considered improper and will cause your website rankings to lower. This applies to using keyword "lists" in your titles, as well as using separate pages for many keyword variants.

Buying backlinks from other sites.

Backlinks are links to your site featured on other websites. These usually come from guest posts, recommendations, endorsements or marketing partnerships you create with other brands. Backlinking is an important strategy in SEO, as it is a factor in proving your credibility as an authoritative site. However, there is a right and a wrong way to get backlinks.

Certain websites will sell backlinks to help your site achieve better rankings. Buying backlinks is another black-hat SEO trick that has long-since been discovered, and is now traceable by Google's crawlers. If your backlinks are not from genuine, reputable sites, you can be penalized in Google's ranking system. Your site can even be removed from the index if enough paid backlinks are discovered.

Irrelevant content.

In the beginning of SEO research and practice, websites would create content around the most trending topics, regardless of whether it was topical to the website itself. You would find "clickbait," or articles with shallow but attention-grabbing titles simply to direct traffic to a site. When the user reached the website, they would then discover that the content they were expecting was not what they were receiving.

Any irrelevant content that could be seen as clickbait should be removed from your site immediately. Use articles and pages that are attention-grabbing, but are still relevant to your site and its purpose.

Meta descriptions.

Google stopped using meta keywords in their ranking factors in 2009. Yet, marketers still obsess over whether enough keywords fit into their meta description, sacrificing quality for SEO. Instead, write your meta descriptions to draw in users rather than focusing on keyword count.

Using microsites or separate domains with the same subject and purpose.

If negative URLs appear for a company's target keywords, some marketers use microsites to try and suppress the content. Microsites are also used to take up SERP space in order to trump the competition. In some cases, if the microsite serves a completely different purpose from the main site (such as a blog or charity project website) it can boost website rankings. However, if the microsite is simply used to hog SERP real estate, your main site may be penalized.

#12

What to Do About a Negative Search Result for Your Company

One of the scariest things for a business to face is bad press. Whether it's a bad review or a negative news article about your company, one poor opinion can spell trouble for your business' short-term sales and long-term customer relationships. And with the rise of online news publications your poor press can be immortalized on the first page of Google.

Your online reputation is crucial because the information sticks long after the article or bad review is published. With news on television and in the paper people soon forget, but online news stays forever and is incredibly difficult to remove entirely. Whenever someone searches for your business name or product, they could find that negative content and change their minds about your business before learning anything else about it.

That is why marketing teams need an online reputation management strategy prepared. One poor review or press release doesn't have to be the end of your otherwise stellar SEO campaign. There are several strategies you can use to make the negative content disappear or become irrelevant in the search engines. But, it takes time and proper strategy to make that negative URL disappear.

An Example of a Ruined Online Reputation

Do you remember the story of Walter Palmer? You probably don't, but you will remember the national controversy he sparked in 2015. Walter Palmer was a dentist in Minnesota with a thriving practice and generally good reputation for his work. But, if you look up "Walter Palmer dentist," his most successful keyword search, you won't find anything about his reputable dental practice.

Palmer was the famed shooter of Zimbabwe's Cecil the Lion. Though he committed no crime, Palmer's name is associated with the evils of trophy hunting and animal abuse. Palmer never expected his private vacation to result in the near death of his career and nationwide public shaming. To this day, negative news articles and social media posts circle his name, ruining his career and reputation anywhere he goes.

The lesson learned with Palmer's story is that 1) online communities are very unforgiving, and 2) a negative online reputation can ruin a career or an entire business. While his case is extreme, the same can happen to your business if a company crisis or negative review catches media attention. There are two options in this scenario: removal of the content and content suppression. Here's how you decide which path to take:

Can you get it removed?

It's uncommon, but sometimes you can have negative content removed permanently if you have the right connections or a legal argument to back you up. Did you post content that received negative comments? Did a friend or acquaintance post something that is negatively affecting your online reputation? If so, these can usually be removed without any harm done to your online reputation.

Google also allows for Takedown requests for certain legal issues. If the negative content fits within their guidelines you may be able to have it removed. However, Google's rules are designed to allow as much freedom as possible for its users so content removal in these circumstances is very hard to achieve. If you can't remove it, you will have to go the route of content suppression in the search engines.

Suppressing negative URLs with new, positive content.

The most effective way to rebuild an online reputation is not to remove, but to bury the negative content in the search results. This is more difficult, especially if the negative content comes from an authoritative site. Negative reviews receive more clicks which boost the rankings. However, if you create an effective ORM strategy, you can suppress this content with your own positive, branded search results.

Step 1. Research your negative search terms. You need to find out what terms and phrases the negative content ranks best for and start targeting those keywords in your ORM campaign. You can use this information to create positive content that will rank for the same terms, burying the negative URL on the second or third pages of the SERPs.

Step 2. Create a content calendar for your negative search terms. Once you've identified the negative search terms, you need to create positive content around the same keywords. The more content you post that competes with the negative content, the more likely it is to go down in the SERP rankings.

Step 3. Post content on your site and other sharing mediums. Posting regularly will help boost your organic rankings and suppress the negative content. Update your website consistently and use the content you create on multiple posting platforms. You can post similar or duplicate content on websites such as Medium without penalty.

Step 4. Share your content on social media. Social profiles rank well for business names and keywords. You want your website, as well as your social media profiles, to outrank the negative search results. The only way for your content to gain traction is for people to see and click on it. Driving traffic to your website through social media will quickly improve the rankings of your positive content.

#13

Repairing the Damage of Bad Online Reviews

When searching for a business online, one of the first things that appears is the Google reviews. Under every business listing is the option for customers to leave their feedback about their experiences. These reviews are public for a reason - other customers want to know as much as they can about a business before making a purchase online because they can't make a judgment call until the product arrives.

Online reviews can be very beneficial to your business. They instill trust in your brand in ways that your company simply cannot. Reviews are unbiased and come directly from advocates of your brand. Even the occasional bad review can be beneficial, as it gives you the opportunity to reach out to an unhappy customer and improve their experience.

However, some customers will not hold back in sharing negative, sometimes uninformed opinions of your brand. These customers can ruin an otherwise stellar online reputation and hurt your sales as long as the review is present. An occasional low rating won't ruin your reputation, but if enough appear online, or if one customer takes their displeasure to multiple platforms, you may be in trouble.

Responding to the Negative Review

When you see a negative review about your business, the first step is to evaluate the problem. Do you remember this customer? Is their complaint a common one or was it based on a one-time mistake from the company? Have they expressed how their expectations were unmet, and if so can you meet them now? You need to empathise with your customers and understand why they left the review before taking further actions.

Once you understand where the customer experience went wrong, you need to plan a way to amend the situation. If they have a specific problem with your product or service, find a way to resolve it. If they were displeased with the customer service, you need to contact them and apologize for your actions. Your customer left this review to warn others about using your company. You need to put these concerns to rest with a long-term solution or else your business will lose credibility.

If you can, find a way to directly contact the writer of the bad review. It's best to take the problem offline and into the hands of your customer service team. That way they don't leave multiple bad reviews online and on social media, making the problem worse. In addition to contacting them directly, you need to respond to the review on the platform it was written.

Your response should show genuine concern and offer the customer a solution and a way to contact your office. You can't just acknowledge the problem, you have to make it clear that they have the option to solve it. If the customer does not contact you, at least they have felt heard. They also have no reason to write another bad review. You're putting the customer in charge, which shows your concern and willingness to help.

Your response should be personal. Use their name if given, and acknowledge their specific complaint. Don't use phrases such as, "We're sorry you were dissatisfied," or "If you have a problem please contact our support." This detaches your brand from your audience, which is not what you want when trying to establish trust.

Rebuilding Trust in Your Brand

Once the problem has been resolved, or you have at least offered a solution, you need to start thinking about how to repair your reputation. If the review was relatively minor, you can move on without much thought about reputation repair. However, if the review has received significant attention, you need to create a plan for reputation repair.

The best way to reduce the impact of a negative review is to drown it with positive reviews. Make an extra effort to ask customers for their feedback. You can send follow up emails directing them to review sites or to your website. You can also send them to your social media profiles where they can leave their feedback. Some online services offer applications to send text messages or emails with links to your review sites. These give customers a prompt to provide you with feedback while the experience is fresh in their minds.

Sometimes a bad review is left on websites such as Ripoff Report, which show up as links in the search engine. These can even outrank your website when customers search for your name, which is bad news for your SEO campaign. These results attract much more attention than they deserve, so you must deal with them immediately.

If negative reviews appears as a search result, you have two options: you can either request to have it removed, or suppress the URL with an aggressive online reputation management (ORM) campaign. ORM usually involves creating content around the keywords that your negative search result ranks for, and suppressing it with more relevant content for the search engine. This can take many months to accomplish, but is the most effective, long-term solution for reputation repair.

The best way to avoid bad reviews online is to take care of the problem before the customer posts about it publicly. Quality customer service and management are key to maintaining a positive reputation on and offline. Follow up with customers after every purchase and you can reduce the amount of poor reviews left online. When a customer has the opportunity to talk with a company representative directly, a bad experience may turn into a good one.

Don't leave your negative reviews unattended. The only way to repair is to accept fault, and work with the customer towards a solution for both of you.

#14

How to Use Instagram for B2B Marketing

Instagram is the world's fastest growing social media platform. While Facebook and Twitter have more users, Instagram gains more users each year than either, and is on track to becoming a leading social media platform for all demographics. The platform provides users with the ability to create stunning photos to share with their friends. It is also a prime advertising and marketing platform for businesses.

Instagram marketing has taken off in recent years, especially for clothing, beauty, and other lifestyle brands. Not only does the app showcase product photos beautifully, but it is most popular among the millennial market. However, this doesn't mean that B2B companies can't benefit from Instagram marketing.

B2B marketing on Instagram isn't meant for lead generation, but rather to develop a community around your brand and share positive brand messages with your fans. Instagram cultivates brand awareness and customer loyalty. It also allows you to venture out of the formal corporate culture and embrace the creative, personable side of your brand.

When you use Instagram for a B2B brand, you need to strike a happy medium between modern and professional. You want to stay true to your brand, but coherent with the platform. Not sure where to start? Here are five different ways you can use Instagram for your B2B marketing:

User generated content.

One of the best ways B2B companies can build trust and brand awareness on Instagram is with user-generated content. Instead of featuring your company products and services, feature your customers using them in action. Include customer testimonials and reviews to add authenticity. Like they say, a picture is worth a thousand words. When users see your clients interacting with your company or using your products, they can visualize the benefit that you could be providing to them.

Wordpress does a tremendous job of incorporating user generated content in their Instagram strategy. They feature photos of entrepreneurs and artists using their sites to further their own creative pursuits. They also use customer testimonials in the form of block quotes to emphasize the overwhelming positivity associates with Wordpress sites.

Company culture.

Another great way for B2B companies to shine on social is to promote their company culture and team. This is not only a smart recruiting tool, but can help build trust with your customers. Companies with happy employees are generally seen as trustworthy and better places of business. Plus, connecting your name to a face helps customers remember your brand.

Have employees featured on your Instagram in their day-to-day work environment. Show them having fun, working hard, and helping customers. You can also have employees take photos themselves, either at the office or in their daily, off-the-clock lives. Showing your employees personalities and sharing their accomplishments is a great way to express your company culture online.

Care about the things your customers care about.

Your Instagram photos don't have to be all about your company. Use photos that represent your company values. You can share quotes, customer or employee success stories and other heartfelt messages on Instagram that your customers will enjoy seeing. Instagram doesn't have to be all about promotion. The most successful pages are authentic and creative, while staying true to brand values.

Share the good things you're doing in the community.

Everyone loves a brand backed by a social cause. If you're involved in a charity partnership or have your own company projects, share about them on Instagram. You can use photos and videos from campaign participants or from involved employees. Show that you're more than just a business - you're an involved part of the community and society.

Humanizing your brand.

Brand personality is just as important in B2B marketing as it is B2C. Your clients need to trust you, and the way to build trust is to develop relationships. Your brand personality can truly shine on Instagram. When writing captions or choosing photos, find ways to incorporate your company story. Use your Instagram account as if it were a personal account.

Instagram stories.

The app recently released a new "Stories" feature, which allows you to add a photo or video to your profile for 24 hours only. The idea behind a story is to share daily snippets without having to keep the picture or video on your page permanently. Instagram stories can help you build an audience and showcase your company culture as your team is hard at work.

Instagram scheduling tools.

Most marketers use scheduling tools for social media marketing. However, scheduling tools for Instagram are not easy to find. The most common are Later, Hootsuite, and Onlypult. These platforms help you plan your Instagram feed, and allow you to upload photos from your desktop. Instagram is an untapped marketing resource for many B2B companies. The sooner you start, the sooner you can create a killer Instagram brand.

#15

How to Make Your Instagram Page Stand Out to Customers

The social media space is overpopulated. Over 500 million active users are on Instagram now, including 2 million business pages. With that much content being produced everyday, it can be hard to make your brand stand out. So difficult in fact, that the average Instagram page has less than 200 hundred followers.

One study on Instagram marketing for 2016 concluded that only about 4.3% of followers interact with business page posts. This means in order to get 100 likes or comments on a post, a page needs approximately 2,325 followers. The average monthly follower increase for Instagram brands is 1.75%, or for a brand of that size, approximately 40 followers a month. To get to that 2,000+ mark takes years of active usage on the app at this rate.

It may seem like Instagram marketing success is nearly impossible to achieve. However, the benefits your brand gains from simply being an active user are worth the effort. Instagram engagement is 58 times higher than Facebook. Top brands (with over 1 million followers) only have to post an average of 4.9 times per week to keep fans engaged. Just one post a day can dramatically increase your visibility to customers, and cultivate brand loyalty over time.

The only way to become a success on Instagram is to dive in. It is the platform where you can best show your brand personality. To make your business stand out among the millions of other business pages, follow these six rules of Instagram marketing:

Optimize your images.

Instagram is all about visuals. The photos you use have to be high-quality or else your business will look unprofessional. Make sure your images are the right size, 1080 px X 1080 ps for square images and 1080 px X 566 px for landscape. Your photos should also follow a visual theme to create coherency. If you use the Instagram filters, choose one or two and stick to them.

Instagram does not allow you to upload photos from a desktop, which can be problematic if you're using professional photos or branded images. However, you can use an Instagram scheduler to work around this.

Use hashtags.

It may seem obvious, but not enough brands effectively use hashtags for their Instagram marketing. Some brands think that hashtags in their posts make them look "cheap" or unprofessional, but the opposite is true. Hashtags are the only way to search. Customers need a way to find your brand based on their interests. Hashtags can also start trends and spread virally if used in conjunction with a promotion or trending conversations.

Post regularly.

Consistency is key. Nearly 70% of photos shared aren't seen because Instagram's feed algorithm is based on engagement, rather than post time or follower count. The more often you post, the more likely people will start recognizing your account and remember your brand. You want to create top-of-mind awareness through social media. The only way to do that is to post on a regular basis. On Instagram, posting once or twice a day is optimal.

Share your Instagram updates on other social media.

You can automatically share your Instagram photos to Facebook and Twitter. Use this to your advantage. The more content you create, the more your overall social media efforts will catch momentum. Plus, Instagram and Twitter hashtags usually coincide in popularity. Something that trends on one app is likely to perform well on the other.

Use Instagram Stories.

Instagram recently released a "Stories" feature similar to that of the Snapchat Story. When you open the app, click on your profile icon in the top left corner, and you can add a photo or take a live video which will show on your profile for 24 hours. They are the perfect way to add personality to your Instagram page, showing your day-to-day work environment and fun things going on in the office.

Showcase your customers.

The best business Instagram pages look like they're regular people's pages. Instead of uploading photos of your product or company, show your customers are using your product or service and benefiting from it in their daily lives. This connects with your followers, as they get to see the real-life benefits of using your product or service, and they may not even notice they're looking at a business page.

Instagram marketing is so important to creating a successful social media campaign. Without Instagram you're missing an entire segment of the market that is right within reach. The more you work on your profile, creating stunning photos and videos for customers to enjoy, the more benefit you can gain for your business.

#16

Habits of Successful Social Media Influencers

In the early 2000s, when social media first became popularized by websites like MySpace and the beginnings of Facebook, no one would've guessed that we would one day be connected globally by social media. Today, over 2 billion of the world's population uses social media in their daily lives. We use these platforms to communicate, express, and influence others in our networks both on and offline.

A social media influencer is someone who has a significant following, especially in a particular industry or niche. They're YouTube stars, active bloggers, activists and professionals who use their experiences and ideas to bring people together for a common interest. Social media influencers work with brands to promote products and ideas to their following.

You don't have to be a celebrity to wield tremendous power on social media. Small brands, as well as everyday people, can make money and grow their fame simply by creating content that users want most. Building a following isn't as easy as it seems, however. Social media marketing for your personal brand is a full time job for successful influencers.

In addition to creating content, influencers must maintain their professional brand everywhere they go. They're in the public eye at all times. Influencers know how to use their personal experiences to grow their professional brand and engage followers on a regular basis. These are their secrets to success:

They maintain their persona on and offline.

Social media influencers are just like celebrities in that their personal lives are out in the open to followers and fans. They must always act with integrity, whether on camera or not. Truly big social media influencers are often under secret watch. Of course you don't have to become a robot with a one-dimensional personality tied to your brand. But, you want to show your fans that you are consistent on and offline.

They constantly network.

To become an influencer, you need to build credibility with your audience. People who are backed by brands and other experts are seen as trustworthy online. Social media influencers don't wait for opportunity; they look for ways to meet new people and gain more followers. They put themselves out there in every way possible.

Twitter and Instagram are the best platforms to give shoutouts and connect with others in your industry. When you reach out to other influencers, they will likely give love back to your brand. Even the biggest stars don't pass up new connections if they add value to their brand. The more value you can add to other influencers' brands, the more they will give back to yours.

They are generous.

Successful influencers are always willing to work with others. The way influencers make money is by gaining endorsements and promoting products for other brands. Most don't get to choose the brands to collaborate with so it's important to have a broad platform. The professionals are ready and willing to promote products that don't always go with their brand if they believe their followers would benefit.

Influencers also use giveaways and free promotions to boost brand popularity. Many companies who choose to work with you will give you free samples of products. It's not a bad idea to use these as gifts for your followers. Many social media users follow brands specifically for giveaway opportunities. This is a quick and easy way to gain followers and hook them on your content.

They spread their efforts across multiple platforms.

Most social media influencers are known for one platform. However, even a strong presence on one platform needs to be supplemented across all social media outlets. Create multiple channels to spread your message. You should be active on a blog or website, and have active profiles for all major social media sites (Facebook, Twitter, LinkedIn, Instagram, and YouTube).

They don't stay the same.

Social media influencers must keep up with trends and stay current in their industry. To do that, they are always reinventing themselves. People want to follow a story and see growth in the individual as they gain fame and new experiences. Stay fresh and up-to-date with the trends to keep your fans engaged. You should always be growing personally and professionally and share those experiences with your followers.

They share their opinions.

One of the hardest parts of being a social influencer is balancing your personal and professional image online. As an influencer, you have the power to inspire and share ideas. However, voicing your opinion on controversial subjects can cause backlash and draw unwanted attention. The best influencers aren't afraid to bring controversial subjects to the table. Your fans are looking to you; they want to know what you think and what you're passionate about.

Becoming a social media star takes time; but, it gives you the platform to share your ideas and make a difference in the world.

#17

7 Things You Should Never Post on Your Business Facebook Page

Facebook can be such a powerful marketing tool for your business or professional brand. It's a place where you can unleash marketing creativity, test brand messaging and connect with your customers in their personal lives. However, the line between personal Facebook use and professional page use can be crossed very quickly.

Some things should NEVER appear on your business Facebook page. No matter how casual or personable you want your brand voice to be, these things are simply not acceptable for a professional image. What you do and post on your personal page is up to your discretion. Whether you're a marketer or business owner, stay away from these 7 Facebook faux pas:

Other page's content (unless you share it).

It can be hard to create content on a daily basis for your Facebook page. Many marketing experts recommend curating, or sharing content from other resources, in order to make up for a lack of original content. However, there is a difference between sharing content from other resources and using it as your own.

This happens most frequently with images and videos. If you do not own the image or video, you need to share it from the original source. If not, you could be stepping on someone else's copyright, which can get your content removed and your page shut down. Sharing, on the other hand, is a great way to network on social media and give your followers fresh content to enjoy.

Racist, sexist or other prejudice humor.

It's surprising how many brands think that racist or sexist humor is appropriate for social media. Even if you think it is innocent, not everyone will appreciate this. Social media isn't a perfect communication tool. People may misinterpret your intentions, taking what is meant to be a joke very seriously. You don't want people to get the wrong impression of your brand.

If you are unsure if a piece of content is offensive, ask a team member or a supervisor for approval. Some racial or gender-sensitive humor is acceptable on social media if it does not demean or discriminate. Always ask for a second opinion before sharing.

Swearing

Some brands can get away with using swear words, but it is very rare. Most of these are media outlets and personal brands that have a very casual brand image. This is not the way to go if you're running a business page or professional-only profile. If you wouldn't swear in front of a customer, you don't need to do it online.

Personal stories and complaints.

Facebook is notorious for being the platform that people use to air their grievances. This is occasionally acceptable on a personal page, but never on a professional one. If followers see you complaining or bringing your personal lives to the business page, you will lose credibility.

Don't overshare either. Some professionals use their business pages to talk about their successes, family lives, and other personal details about their lives. Sometimes this is appropriate, but this doesn't add value for your followers. Most of the time this will be seen as unprofessional and will drive away customers.

Political or religious opinions.

Being involved in social and environmental issues is appropriate for some brands, but aligning yourself with a political party or figure is very dangerous. You'll end up alienating many customers, no matter which side you choose. Political talk is frowned upon on personal pages, and should never appear on your professional profiles either.

The same applies to religion. Unless you are managing a page for a nonprofit or business with a religious background, the topic should not be discussed.

Asking followers to "Like" your page or status.

Like-gathering posts are overused and annoying to most followers. They don't encourage engagement - in fact they often have the opposite effect. If the person is seeing the post, they've already liked your page. They don't need to be asked again. If you create good content the likes will come. Asking for likes comes across as aggressive and desperate.

The only time it is appropriate to ask for likes is if your page is running a contest based on post engagement. Asking customers to like a post in order to enter a giveaway is a great way to boost engagement, but asking them to like a post without incentive simply won't work.

Photos of your customers without their permission.

Sure, some customers will be flattered that you featured them on your business page. But, some will be angered or embarrassed. They may ask you to take the photo down or report it. You need explicit permission before you post a photo of a customer, and should show them the photo as a courtesy before posting it online. The same rule applies to employees.

Hopefully, you haven't made any of the mistakes on this list. When in doubt, always air on the side of caution when posting to your Facebook page.

#18
How to Conduct an SEO Audit For Your Website

Optimizing your website for the search engines is the most important aspect of your online marketing initiatives. A high-performing website is the backbone of all other campaigns. A high-performing site drives traffic, converts leads, and generates buzz on social media. Everything else is secondary to your SEO campaign, for it gives momentum to all other strategies you can use to market online.

60% of website clicks come from the top organic search results, not pay-per-click ads. Ranking at the top of the search engines gives credibility to your brand. However, getting to that point is no easy task. Thousands of other business are optimized for the same audience that you're trying to reach. In order to beat out the competition, you need to constantly update your SEO strategies and stay current with Google's algorithm changes.

SEO strategy can be divided into three core competencies: technical optimization, content creation, and competitive analysis. Taking the time to audit your website for these three areas can save you a lot of frustration long-term.

Keyword analysis

Keywords are the foundation of SEO. The search terms your customers are using should be the framework for your content. The better optimized your site is for high-use keywords, the more traffic you can drive to your site over the competition.

Keyword analysis can be broken into two parts: finding which keywords are bringing your site the most traffic, and what words are most used by your audience that you are not currently ranking for. Different tools will help you identify these keywords, which you can then use to create your content and make changes to your site.

You need to know which keywords will bring the greatest ROI for your SEO campaign. First, you will want to see what is already ranking for your branded and non-branded search terms. To do this, make a list of the keywords you are trying to target. Search each of them and make a second list to see 1) if your site ranks on the SERPs for these words, and 2) what other sites also rank for your target keywords.

Second, you want to see which keywords are bringing the most traffic to your site. Tools like SEMRush will give you a list of words that Google associates with your content, so you are able to know how customers are finding your site most frequently. You can find the top-ranking pages on your site by searching "site:*yourdomain*.com." The top-ranked pages on your site will appear in the search results. Keywords on these pages are the highest-performing.

Knowing where your SEO campaign is strongest, and which keywords you need to be targeting can help you create a stronger content plan and further shape your SEO strategy to get the best ROI for the keywords you choose to target.

Be careful, however, about overusing the same keywords in all of your content. This is called "keyword cannibalization," when two or more pages on your site compete for the same spot in the SERPs for a keyword. Each of your core pages should be optimized for a different keyword or phrase as to avoid duplicate or competing content.

Technical analysis

The technical aspects of your SEO are just as important as your content strategy. During your audit you should do a website crawl for technical errors. These are the most common SEO technical errors that can slow down your progress:

- Canonicalization errors and redirects
- Broken links
- Sparse or duplicate content
- Problems in sitemap navigation
- Slow load speeds
- Lack of a responsive mobile version for your site
- Missing or non-optimized metadata

Each of these errors can significantly impact your rankings, so it's best to fix them right away. A high-performance site creates a better user experience, and is easier for the search engines to crawl a site with all of these elements in working order.

Competitor analysis

Optimizing your site for keywords isn't enough. You have to outrank competitors with superior content, a greater number of backlinks, and an overall higher-functioning website. Knowing your competitors' successes can help you reverse engineer their strategies for your own advantage.

Using your keyword list, find out which competitors are top-ranked, and identify the pages that perform best for them. You can conduct a simple search or use more advanced tools like SEMRush and Google Analytics to find your answers.

One of the biggest mistakes SEO marketers make is trying to compete for competitors' branded search terms with PPC ads. This black-hat SEO trick may boost traffic, but it will hurt your reputation and is not the best use of your resources. You want to outrank competitors, but you need to earn that position, not buy it.

#19

Reasons Your Website Doesn't Rank on Google

Search engine optimization is the collection of practices marketers use to increase website traffic through organic search engine results. Search engines, like Google and Bing, help users locate sites based on their interests through a complex algorithm that matches keywords to quality content. Web developers, in turn, can optimize their pages to meet the algorithm's criteria and receive more traffic from the search engine results.

Improving a website's user experience increases its credibility, which helps it "rank" higher in the search results. A higher ranking means more clicks, and therefore more leads to capitalize on. Search engine optimization has a significantly higher ROI than pay-per-click or even social media advertising because you don't have to pay for any of the traffic. The only investment you need to make is time and recruiting the best SEO marketers to your team to make your campaign a success.

There are many different ways to optimize your website and increase its rankings, but even the best efforts may not be enough if any of these issues are present on your website.

Your content is too short.

For pages to rank well, they need to give the search engine plenty of content. Content is the only way search engine crawlers can identify keywords and decipher the theme and subjects your website covers. The more copy present per page, the more keywords a search engine crawler can identify and use to rank your site. Search engines prefer long-form copy because it is more beneficial to users and to their algorithms.

On average, the top ten search results presented are 2000+ words. These are what SEO specialists call "pillar posts," as they are the foundation for your content marketing strategy. Without pillar posts, your content doesn't have any authority. While short blog posts are easy to create on a regular schedule, make time for long-form content to boost your site authority.

You have spelling errors or duplicate content on your site. Grammar issues give site visitors a very poor first impression. Search engines look for spelling errors and glaring grammatical mistakes and place those sites lower in the search results. If too many errors occur on your site, it may be penalized or removed from the search engine index. Before you post anything make sure to run it through a grammar-checking tool.

Duplicate content can also cause problems for your website rankings. If you post the same page more than once or on another website, it confuses the search engine on which page to rank higher. Usually, the search engine will choose to penalize both sites and the content won't be seen at all. Even small snippets of duplicate content can cause major problems for your site.

Page errors.

Small technical errors are bound to happen on any website, and the search engines won't penalize you for these. However, if a page has been removed or experiences long-term problems, but still appears in your site's navigation, you may be penalized.

- 403 Error - The user has tried to access a page that is forbidden

- 404 Error - The user tries to access a page that is no longer available
- 500 Error - A general error caused by the internal server

If you have a 403, 404 or 500 error on your site, it simply won't rank, no matter how good the rest of your content is. These errors create a poor user experience and lower the credibility of your site to web crawlers.

Your site is not mobile friendly.

Google recently switched to a "mobile first" algorithm for ranking. This means they use the mobile version of a site for indexing and ranking before the desktop version. Mobile optimization is a core element of SEO best practice, and if your website is not optimized for mobile, you can't expect to be ranked at the top page for any search engine.

You have a high bounce rate.

The bounce rate of a site is the percentage of visitors who leave your site after visiting just one page. A high bounce rate indicates that your content is not relevant to users or not engaging enough to keep them reading. The less time people spend on your site, the less likely you are to rank well. Make sure your visitors have plenty of content to view and direct them from one place to the other to keep them on your page.

You haven't submitted your sitemap to Google Webmaster Tools.

Google crawlers use the sitemap to quickly scan your content for the information they need to categorize and rank your site for keywords. The crawlers search for sites all across the web, but it helps if you send your sitemap to Google Webmaster Tools directly. This will help Google find your site and start indexing pages for the right keywords.
Luckily, any of these SEO mistakes can be easily resolved with some minor changes to your site. The more you learn, the better your SEO campaign will perform and the more quality leads you'll be able to generate from search engine marketing.

#20
Social Media Cliches You Shouldn't Use in Your Marketing

Social media is one of the more creative and fun parts of any marketing campaign. Social media is a platform where you can express your brand voice in a personable way to customers. You can also use it to experiment with modern media and bring your brand to life in all types of digital media.

Social media should be the place where you take your most imaginative marketing ideas. It should be your platform to create new, not just follow the rules. There's no reason to play it safe on social media. The more creative you are, the more your brand will stand out in the minds of customers. Creativity wields tremendous power.

Though we can't always create groundbreaking content for our social profiles, there are a few types of posts that are simply overused and should never appear on your page. These posts will be ignored by your audience and give a bad impression for your brand. Avoid using these cliches on any social media platform:

"Like our page" posts.

Asking for likes for your page or post is cliche and annoying for your audience. First, if they are seeing your posts, it's likely they've already liked your page and the post adds no value. Even if they have not, telling your customers to like a page gives them no incentive to actually do so. You can't tell your audience what to do - you have to give them reason to like your page or post.

What's the best way to get more likes and engagement for your page? Share content of quality. There is no replacement for good work and a strong brand identity.

Memes.

Humor is a powerful tool on social media. However, not all types of humor are appropriate for your business page. Memes, cat videos, and the like are cliche, and don't add any value to your brand. Unless the humor is specific to your business or industry, it doesn't need to be shared on your business page. Humor on social media should be clever and creative. You can't build an audience on recycled memes and low-level humor that every other page uses.

Inspirational quotes.

Social media can be a platform to inspire your audience. Inspirational stories, especially shared through video, are powerful tools used to engage your audience and start a trend online. This type of content evokes emotion in your audience which connects them to your brand. Inspirational content is highly effective on social media, but inspirational quotes are not.

Inspirational quotes are overused, uncreative, and a clear sign that your social media strategy isn't unique. Unless the quote comes from you or your company founder, you shouldn't post it on your business page. Reposting a quote from someone famous, even if they're in your industry, isn't creative. It's boring. Never make your page look boring with stereotypical inspirational quotes.

Holiday posts.

Yes, marketing during the holidays is important. You should be promoting sales, leveraging holiday trends, and joining the celebration with your audience. However, if you're going to start a holiday marketing campaign, you need to commit to it. No irrelevant posts wishing everyone a "happy holiday," unless you're willing to back that up with real, valuable content. You don't need to post for every holiday either, unless it is important to your community.

Types of Posts that are Anything But Cliche

On social media, anything goes. As long as the content you use is original, branded and relevant to your audience, you can do anything and everything you want with your campaign.

These types of content perform exceptionally well on social media. If you're looking for something to add a spark to your content calendar, try these four types of social media posts:

- **User generated content** - If you need more original content, don't just look to your marketing department. Ask customers for photos of themselves using your products or services. This is a definitive way to prove your worth to other potential customers.

- **Livestreams** - Facebook recently added a new "Live" feature, which allows you to broadcast live videos from your phone onto your page. Not enough brands utilize Facebook Live for its potential to attract viewers and keep them engaged rather than scrolling through the feed.

- **VR product demos** - Virtual Reality is at the forefront of marketing technology. When customers can see firsthand the capabilities of a product or experience something with a brand from the comfort of their own homes, they gain trust and interest in your brand. Even GoPro videos and experiences can provide customers with a unique experience on social that connects them to your company.

- **Stories** - Snapchat, Instagram, and Facebook all have "story" features, where you can add photos and short videos to your page for a 24-hour period. These stories give customer a glimpse into the daily life of your office, and can be a fun, uplifting way to engage with customers.

#21

6 Tools to Aid Your SEO Campaign

For a marketer, tracking and analyzing are pertinent to success online. In order to understand if our efforts create value, we have to monitor progress more than any other department in a business. Search engine optimization is one of those areas that require intense monitoring and analytics. These six tools will help you improve your SEO campaign and track your progress along the way.

SEMRush

- **What it does:** SEMRush provides extensive analytics reports on domains, keywords, and URLs. It provides information for both organic and paid search results, including keyword match lists, cost-per-click data, backlinks, and top results for keywords.

- **What is costs:** Between $100 and $400 monthly

SEMRush is a one-stop shop for SEO research. It can be used for keyword targeting. You can track results of SEO and ORM campaigns across multiple data indicators. SEMRush can help you build better SEO strategies based on analysis of your own and competitor websites and advertising. You can even track social media performance or compare domain data with your competitors' sites.

SEMRush is a wonderful tool, but comes at a steep price. If you are creating analytics reports for clients or have many different websites you need to maintain, it's a wise investment. However, for singular businesses looking for low-cost SEO management tools, this platform may be more than necessary.

Ahrefs

- **What it does:** Ahrefs tracks all of your website data from you highest performance keywords to your site ranking for different Google SERPs. Ahrefs provides domain comparisons so you can reverse engineer your competitors SEO tactics.

- **What is costs:** Between $100 and $1000 monthly

Ahrefs is a professional-level SEO tool designed to help you manage your campaigns and compare data of yours and your competitors' sites. You can also run a complete site audit to pinpoint SEO problems and fix them. You can search for the most popular content on any subject, by backlinks, social shares and organic traffic.

Ahrefs is perfect for small businesses with in-depth SEO strategies in place. It is also a capable tool for marketing agency reporting and SEO.

Buffer

- **What it does:** Buffer is a social media scheduling tool, compatible with Facebook, Pinterest, Instagram, LinkedIn, and Twitter. You can schedule posts months in advance, and track your engagement across all platforms.
- **What is costs:** Up to $400, with a free plan and custom pricing options

Buffer is one of the most popular social media schedulers available. It is intuitive, allows for scheduling far in advance, and has no limits to the number of posts you can create with the upgraded plans. Buffer also tracks your analytics and can produce reports for your different profiles.

Buffer can be a useful SEO tool to see how well your content is performing on social, and how much traffic you're driving to your site via social channels. Plus, it offers plans for every budget, so any business or entrepreneur can use it.

Google Search Console

- **What it does:** Search Console allows website owners to see how their sites are indexing and gain information about their site's visibility and ranking on Google.
- **What is costs:** Free

Google Search Console, formerly referred to as Webmaster Tools, allows you to submit your sitemap for indexing, check statuses, and receive updates on penalties that your site has received according to Google's ranking algorithm. The Search Console is the best tool to help your site start ranking in the search engines and to find errors that you can fix on your site.

Google Analytics

- **What it does:** Google Analytics tracks organic and paid website traffic and learns about your audience's behaviors and changes. It connects to your ad account if you choose to run PPC ads and will give you real-time updates on the progress of your campaign.

- **What is costs:** Free

Every marketer needs to use Google analytics for website traffic monitoring. It is the most accurate tool for measuring your SEO success in organic and paid search traffic. Google adds a tracking code to your website so they can monitor new visitors, your bounce rate, and all other factors that are essential to better understanding SEO.

#22
How to Write a Better Blog Post

You probably already know how important blogging is to your digital marketing campaign. It's the source of your content for social media, it's what drives organic traffic to your website, and without it, your SEO strategy has no foundation. A well executed blog can lead to hundreds or even thousands of new site visitors and can generate leads for your business without any active management.

The problem is, how do you make your blog better than average? You may have blog content on your site, but is it really doing the job? Can you say that your blog generates online leads on a regular basis? If you're unsure, the answer is probably no. A blog can't do its job if 1) you don't have a strategy to promote it, or 2) your content isn't strong enough to attract leads.

Writing blog content is tricky. You need to present your information from a different angle because thousands of other websites are competing for the same traffic. A blog does no good to your SEO strategy if it isn't seen. To get those clicks, you need content that stands out among the rest.

These are some tips to help you create better content for your blog and website. Focus on these areas to improve your writing, and get more traffic from your content marketing strategy:

Write in phases.

In school, you were taught to plan, write and revise essays before turning them into the teacher. The same rule applies for professional writing and blogging. Professional content writers usually write two or three drafts of their work before finally publishing it. You should do the same. If you put as much effort into planning and editing as you do the writing of your blog, you will have a much more compelling and coherent final product.

Start with a title, then create an outline for your post. Next you can fill in the details, writing notes, facts and elements you want to use in your copy. Once your notes and ideas are rewritten into paragraphs, edit them for clarity. Finally, send your work to an editor or coworker for final revisions. Then you're ready to publish.

Focus on the intro.

Usually the intro of a blog is the weakest part. The hard part of writing a blog is getting started.. Once you have a few sentences and a direction for your writing, it's easier to fill in the details. That is why blog intros usually suffer. They're incoherent, cliche, or so vague that they don't compel the reader to move on to the meat of the content.

If you can't think of a good introduction, use some of these ideas:
- Lead with a statistic relating to your content
- Tell the reader a story
- Define the term or concept that your blog post is about

Give all the details.

Google ranks pages with more content higher than pages with shorter copy. On average, the top three search results contain 2000+ words, plus visual content. Google may not use word count as an exact ranking factor, but longer content usually contains more keywords and gives the search engine a better understanding of the concepts and subjects contained in your post. The more information you can give that is relevant, the better your blog will perform in search engines.

You may think 2000 words is too much for one blog post, but the content will accumulate faster than you think. If you're having trouble adding that much relevant detail, look for statistics, studies, or other relevant facts online that can boost your content's authority.

Break up your sections.

On average, a reader will spend less than a minute per blog post they click on. People want to scan your content for the information they're looking for. They don't want to have to read pages and pages of content searching for the one thing that they need. To help your readers, use headers, lists, and short, easily-digestible "chunks" of information to break up your blog post, both visually and contextually. Each paragraph should be three to five sentences long, no more.

Hide "Easter eggs" in your blog.

Most blog posts share one common problem - they're boring. They say the same thing in the same way as every other blog. Readers get bored, and therefore don't take the time to read your content and truly learn from it. You may not be able to create a stellar post every time; but, if you can sneak one clever line in every piece of content you write, you'll quickly start winning more fans for your blog.

Add visual content.

Your blog doesn't have to be all writing. Adding infographics, photos, and videos will improve your content and reduce bounce rates. You can use custom graphics, photos you take yourself, or simply stock photos you find online. Make sure you optimize your images so they're the correct size and look right on both mobile and desktop versions of your site.

#23
What to Know About Google SEO Updates of 2017

The Google search engine is possibly one of the world's most powerful tools. On average, Google runs over 40,000 search queries per second. That's close to 3.5 billion searches every single day. Google has reigned over all other search engine tools because it provides the best experience for users worldwide. Their algorithms provide most accurate results and are updated for user compatibility hundreds of times each year.

Not all updates are major, but over time they develop into the major changes we've seen to improve their user experience. Before we discuss the 2017 algorithm changes, let's look at a brief history of Google's updates over the past 15 years.

History of Google Algorithm Updates from 2011 to 2016:

- **Panda Update 2011** - First of many updates to remove sites that use keyword stuffing or other SEO tactics that lowered quality of content for better rankings.
- **Penguin Update of 2012** - Removed sites found whose backlinks were paid or coming from "link farm" sites.
- **Pirate Update of 2012** - Added a filter to the algorithm to rid the top search results of sites with copyright infringement complaints or reports.
- **Exact Match Domain Update of 2012** - Removes poor quality sites from ranking well in the SERPs simply because the domain matches the search query.
- **Top Heavy Update of 2012** - Removed sites with excessive banner and sidebar ads from top search results.
- **Hummingbird Update of 2013** - The Hummingbird update improved the engine's ability to "understand" or match a keyword's meaning and context to sites

most related, rather than focusing on the quality of keyword matches found on the page.
- **Payday Update of 2013** - Intended to improve the quality of search results for queries traditionally associated with spammy or untrustworthy sites, such as payday loans or gambling sites.
- **Pigeon Update of 2014** - Changed ranking factors and improved distance parameters for local search listings to give users better quality results for local listings.
- **Mobile-Friendly Update 2015** - This changed Google's algorithm to rank sites based on their mobile versions before their desktop versions, and boosted sites that follow Google's mobile-friendly best practices.

2017 Major Updates

Fred - The Fred update was launched in March of 2017. It made major improvements to Google's semantic search ranking and quality control of content for the SERPs. The Fred update targeted sites with low-quality pages, mostly those used for affiliate marketing or promotional purposes only. This means that if your site is cluttered with short-form, non-informative pages, it could be penalized and lose ranking to sites with longer, more quality pages and posts.

The Fred update is part of Google's push for better content and user experiences. Google no longer wants to direct users to sites with short or promotional-only material. They are continually working on the search engine's semantic search capabilities. The Fred update is part of this drive towards higher expectations for website content from both the users and the search engines.

Hawk - The Hawk update, released in August 2017, made a major impact on local search rankings. It changed the way Google's algorithms filter out local search results and made a major impact on local SEO across all industries.

Some background on the Hawk update: Google filters search results by finding similar content across different local listings. They choose the most relevant content for each local listing to rank at the top and filter out the rest of the content to avoid two top search results from the same site. This keeps local search results fair and impartial so that one monster site doesn't take up all the SERP space.

The Hawk update changed the algorithm for local listings. Now, instead of filtering out pages by their domain or address, the engine will filter out pages with websites that share a close geographical region. This means that if a competitor is close to you on Google maps, your site (or theirs) can be filtered out of the top search results. While this turned out to be problematic for some businesses, it made for a better user experience and upped the game for local SEO.

Minor updates

Snippet Length Increase - Google increased meta description length to 300 characters. This allows for more space for a company's call to action.

Intrusive Interstitial Penalty - An interstitial is a popup or display ad that is presented before a user can view desired content. Usually these pop-ups are used to a) confirm age of the user, b) display an ad, or c) ask users to sign up for an email list or promotion. Google now penalizes sites with aggressive interstitial usage if it is deemed harmful to the user experience.

Google's algorithm updates not only help users, but provide incentive for marketers to improve their content and innovate their marketing strategies. Google provides marketers with information on their algorithms to always stay current and follow best practices for better rankings. The more you know, the better you can optimize your site for search engines.

Although these updates have made the user experience better, they continue to frustrate marketers, as these updates change the effectiveness of SEO strategies.

#24
Beginner Graphic Design Tools Anyone Can Use

Some people say you can't make money in the arts, that visual art and design won't pay the bills no matter how talented you are. These people don't know graphic designers. A graphic designer is the artist behind a brand. They create the beauty behind an advertising campaign. Without graphic designers, our business world would be a colorless place.

Graphic design is one of the most valuable skill sets to have as a marketer, freelancer or entrepreneur. So much of marketing is based on visual elements. Graphic designers are needed for branding, creating print and digital marketing materials, and to create visual assets for websites and social media.

At some point in your marketing career, you'll need to create a brochure, website page or infographic for a project. It's best to have the elemental skills to create these on your own, rather than hiring out every time you take on a new project. Even if you aren't a graphic designer, you can still learn the basics from these online tools and programs:

Canva

Canva is a great beginner's tool for graphics and photo editing. It offers templates for social media posts (with optimal dimensions), official documents, marketing materials, and more. Canva also has an extensive library of pre-made illustrations, photos, and generic shapes that you can use in your graphic designs. Canva is easy to learn and gives users all the tools they need to create professional graphics and illustrations.

Canva's basic plan is free to use, and includes 1GB of storage for photos, over 8,000 templates, and a library of stock photos available for only $1 each. Canva for Work is only $12.95 per month, and with the upgrade you can access several premium design features. You can resize designs with one click, add custom color palettes for your brand, and use exclusive free stock photos from Canva. It's the perfect beginner's tool for social media and website graphic design.

Piktochart

Piktochart is a graphic design tool used for infographics, presentations, and printable marketing materials for your business. The interface is user-friendly and easy to learn. Piktochart gives users thousands of templates to choose from and free icons and images for customization. Piktochart can also create graphs and charts from your data to illustrate information on your website, a brochure, or any other medium you need.

Piktochart's basic version is free to use, but they have premium packages ranging from $15 to $30, depending on the features you need and the number of team members you need to invite. They also have special packages for educational and nonprofit use.

Pixlr

Pixlr is an all-encompassing photo editing tool for desktop and mobile applications. Pixlr has four different tools, and a Chrome extension that is customized for different photo editing functions and purposes. The five Pixlr products include:

- **Pixlr Today** - Chrome extension that provides you with beautiful background photos, quotes, weather information, and a personal to-do list tool. When you download the extension you can access Editor and O-Matic functions in one click from your browser.

- **Editor** - Photo editor for desktop, includes all basic Pixlr photo editing tools.
- **O-Matic** - Edit photos for vintage or retro style.
- **Express** - Allows you to add filters, stickers, and has basic editing features to give photos their best possible form and style.
- **Mobile Pixlr** - Crop, edit, and add filters to photos and images on your mobile device.

GIMP

GIMP was the first graphics and image editor of its time. The software is open-source, meaning it is free to the public to edit and use. GIMP is primarily used for image retouching, drawing and image format conversions (similar to the Windows Paint app), however it's extensive toolkit for editing gives users an open canvas to create and design.

GIMP software is developed and maintained by volunteers, so it is now and always will be free to use. While GIMP is free, it is more complex to use and learn. Some practice is necessary before beginners can use it as a graphic design tool.

Adobe illustrator

Adobe Illustrator is the standard software for professional graphic designers. It creates high quality images and downloads and has all the tools necessary for complex designs. While Illustrator is a professional-level tool, beginners can still use it and learn the basics quickly. Not all Adobe tools are difficult to learn. If you plan on creating custom graphics such as logos or website icons, Adobe Illustrator is the best tool to use. However, it is more expensive than web-based applications.

#25
How To Market Yourself As A Freelancer Online

Most of us dream of one day becoming our own boss. For some, that means owning a business. Others take the path of freelancing, a self-employed career path where you are tied to no business entity or employer. Freelancers are highly-skilled workers who find their own clients, set their own rates for work, and control most other aspects of their work life.

Freelancing is appealing to those who enjoy working by themselves and controlling most of their work life. You get to choose how many projects you take on, when you set your work hours, and what services you will or will not provide. Freelancing provides a great deal of freedom, but requires a strong work ethic and self-management skills to be successful.

Freelancing can be a very rewarding career path, but it requires more work upfront than a regular job would. You have to train yourself, find clients by your own initiative, and manage your work tasks without help from a team, coworkers, or a boss. To start your freelancing career right, here are five different ways to find your first clients and start making money:

Define your target market first.

Just like any other business, freelancers have to select the best customer segments and target them to gain more clients. You should have a clear idea of where you want to take your freelancing career and what type of work suits you best. Once you decide what type of work you want to do, you need to find the right customers who could best benefit from your service.

If you're not sure who you're marketing to, you won't be able to select the best channels to send your marketing message out. Though freelancers can take on any type of client, it's best to focus your efforts on the most profitable types of work. You may also consider specialization in a niche in your field. The more specialized your services, the more you can charge per hour or project. This will also help you use your time wisely in finding the best clients for your business.

Create social media profiles.

It's no secret that many employers use the internet to research candidates for jobs. This is even more true with subcontractors, as they are responsible for their own work and not directly supervised by the company. A freelancer's reputation, both personally and professionally, plays a crucial role in whether they can close the deal with clients or not.

One easy way to boost your online reputation and make yourself visible to companies searching for freelancers is creating social media profiles for your business. Having a professional LinkedIn and Facebook page will make it easier for potential clients to find you and gives them your basic information to contact you.

Write a blog about your field.

If you want to be a freelancer, you need to distinguish yourself not only as a professional, but an expert in your field. In the beginning it will be hard to build a reputation. If you don't have clients yet, there's no one to vouch for your quality of work or knowledge in the field.

However, you can show your depth of knowledge to prospective clients and prove yourself as a trusted resource through blogging about your field. Blogs are educational for clients, can build your reputation, and if written well, can convince some prospects to contact you for hire.

Networking and prospecting.

Every freelancer needs to have strong networking skills in order to acquire clients. While online traffic will produce some leads, it may not be enough to make a living on freelancing alone. Everywhere you go, you should be looking for potential clients and needs you can fill in the community. To expand your network and improve your prospecting skills, you need to:

- Find the people you want to connect with in your business community
- Reach out and introduce yourself to contacts as a friend and fan of their work
- Build rapport and trust with your most important contacts
- Follow up with them consistently so you're the first person that comes to mind when they need a service like yours

Your client recommendations should be your primary marketing tool.

Starting out, you'll need to hustle for clients and put your name out there for as many jobs as you can handle. However, as you start to grow your portfolio and gain recurring clients, you can use their networks as a source for more clients. All it takes is one happy client to spread the word, and soon you'll have enough work from referrals that you don't need to go gig hunting.

Whenever you complete a project for a client, follow up with them to ensure they are happy with your work. If they send positive feedback, ask them for a referral directly. If they don't have any referrals to send right away, ask them to leave a review on your freelancer profiles or website. If you have your own professional website, it's a good idea to have a testimonials page or section so that you can send these recommendations to prospective clients.

The appeal to freelance is irresistible for some of us. Who wouldn't want to be their own boss and build their own career from scratch? While a freelancer career isn't easy, the benefits are truly worth the effort. As long as you pursue your leads and deliver quality work, you'll have no trouble launching a very successful freelance career.

#26
Social Media Schedulers You Can Use for Free

Social media is at the forefront of digital marketing. Every business, whether a mom and pop shop or major corporation, needs a social media presence. Customers look for a business' social media accounts if they want to find contact information, share a review, or learn more about a product or service. Social media also gives customers a platform to connect with your brand on a personal level. Without it, your company will give the impression that is not current with marketing initiatives and may lose potential customers to other social-savvy competitors.

Social media is also a valuable research tool for your business. Most social media platforms give you detailed analytics to learn who your best customers are, how they react and engage with your brand, and what social strategies work best for you. Social media is the fastest, free and most accurate way to conduct market research of your own.

With all this emphasis on social media marketing, your business needs the tools to create a strategized social feed. Here are some of the best scheduling tools to keep your accounts up-to-date and track your social stats:

Buffer

- **What You Can Use It For:** Twitter, Facebook, LinkedIn, Pinterest, and Instagram (limited)
- **Pricing:** Free use, premium plans range from $10 - $400 per month

Buffer is one of the most popular social media schedulers for in-house marketing teams and small social media marketing companies. In Buffer, you can manage multiple accounts and brands, and create custom posts for all major social media platforms. Buffer also makes it easy to schedule updates months in advance. It tracks your analytics, giving you data that the platforms don't always track on business pages.

Buffer has multiple plans to fit any budget. Their free version limits the accounts you can connect and the number of posts you can schedule, but all the features are available. If you want to add more accounts or schedule more than 10 posts, you can upgrade to their Awesome plan, which allows you to connect up to ten social accounts and add up to 100 posts at a time. If you're looking to manage one personal or business' social media, Buffer is the best option for you.

Hootsuite

- **What You Can Use It For:** Facebook, Twitter, Wordpress, YouTube
- **Pricing:** 30 day free trial, $19/mo to $500/mo for premium features

Hootsuite is the choice for professionals and small businesses who want to manage their own social accounts, curate content and create more unique social posts for their pages. Hootsuite is more expensive, and the tools are more complex than Buffer's platform. However, they give more detailed analytics reports and offer additional features such as RSS feeds and social media contest templates. Hootsuite also offers unlimited scheduling for their basic plan, while Buffer only allows this for their premium members.

Facebook

- **What You Can Use It For:** Facebook only
- **Pricing:** Free with optional ad features

If your primary social platform is Facebook, you can skip the third party schedulers and plan posts directly on your page. Scheduling a post on Facebook is just like creating one, and you can schedule as many posts of any kind (including photos, articles, and even ads) in advance. Your scheduled posts will show up under the Business Manager tab on your homepage.

Scheduling directly on Facebook gives you several advantages. First, you know your posts will turn out exactly as you've composed them. Some scheduler tools don't translate perfectly to the platform, which means your posts may look differently on the page than they did when you created them. Plus, you can't boost posts that come from Buffer or Hootsuite. If you want to schedule a boosted post, you can do so on Facebook.

TweetDeck

- **What You Can Use It For:** Twitter Only
- **Pricing:** Free

TweetDeck is the premier scheduler for Twitter accounts. Once an independent app, TweetDeck was acquired by the platform and is promoted by Twitter for individuals and enterprises alike. TweetDeck is free to use and there are no premium plans or features. It allows you to schedule, monitor, and track analytics for multiple Twitter accounts. According to Twitter, it is the most popular scheduling tool for its platform.

Small businesses and major corporations alike use TweetDeck. Because it is owned by Twitter, it is perfectly optimized for post sharing and provides real-time analytics on your pages. The interface is easy to learn and incredibly valuable for keeping your Twitter accounts up to date.

Each of these schedulers can help you stay on top of your social media marketing plan. The most important aspect of any social media marketing strategy is consistency. For your accounts to gain followers you need to post relevant content on a daily basis. These tools can help you organize your content and keep your pages up-to-date at all times.

#27

How to Set Up a Content Calendar

A content calendar, or editorial calendar, is used by publishers, bloggers, and businesses to strategize content marketing across multiple platforms. Content calendars help teams stay organized and plan comprehensive content that give their readers real value. Without one, most content marketing strategies are ineffective. They are not planned effectively and follow no clear vision or path to achieving any goals.

By using a content calendar, you'll never miss the opportunity for seasonal content or important updates. The editor or leader of your content marketing team can collaborate with team members more effectively. Plus, you'll gain a better understanding of your own strategy by laying out in weekly or monthly increments. Using a content calendar is elementary for marketing success, and the setup process is easy. Here's what you need to do:

Step 1. Research

Many businesses have weak content marketing strategies because their content is shallow and sales-y, offering no real value to the customer visiting the page. Businesses recycle cliche content ideas because they believe that "clickbait" titles will actually sell. This is far from the reality. Content marketing can't be done right unless your topics are useful to customers and provide unique insight they can't get anywhere else.
Before you start writing, you need to research your target market. Find the most searched keywords in your industry, then create content surrounding those inquiries. Research trends in your industry, including new technologies and controversies that your business can provide insight for readers. The more you know about your customers and their needs, the better content ideas and writing you'll be able to produce.

Step 2. Audit

Before creating new content, go through the existing content on your website. Compare site pages and blogs to see what is best performing and what needs improvement. This will give you a better idea of what you want your future content to look like and which strategies in your campaign are working best. You may also want to rewrite core pages on your website if they have high bounce rates or don't convert at the rate you'd like them to.

A comprehensive SEO audit can help you optimize your website for the best user experience. Fixing bugs and optimizing content based on your research will help your site receive better rankings in the search engines. It will also increase the click-through-rate (CTR) of your website. When a user finds one informational page or article, they'll be more likely to scan your site looking for more.

Step 3. Bookmark Important Dates

Planning out content a week or a month in advance gives you the advantage. You can create better posts surrounding important events and sales, rather than trying to create a promotional campaign last-minute. This will also help your marketing team stay organized and communicate about campaign highlights or specials you want to promote. As you're planning your content, mark dates where you'll want to create special content, such as for:

- All holidays
- Seasonal sales
- Product launches
- Company events
- Special campaigns or projects
- Company milestones

Step 4. Write Out Your Content Ideas

Start with writing the titles of articles or videos you plan to share over the week or month you're planning with your content calendar. If you are planning for the next month, write 30 titles for one article, video, or share each day. Knock out any content surrounding the important dates you bookmarked. Then fill in the rest with content that your research shows will perform well.

To keep track of your titles, keep an index of content for every week or month. You can refer to this index later on to avoid creating duplicate content or overusing an idea. This index can also help you keep track of page links, date posted, and any other information your team might need to keep for reference.

Step 5. Plan Each Day

Once you have all of your titles written, plan out your posting and sharing schedule on the calendar. Ideally, you'll plan a day to post all of your content on your website, or have each post planned for two days - one to create, and one to post and share. You can also write notes to comment, post images, and curate content for your social feeds. Each day should have a clear plan of what needs to be accomplished.

A content calendar will change the way you execute your content and social media marketing strategies. Having a plan in place will not only strengthen your overall strategy, it will help your team communicate and curate novel ideas for your content marketing plan. If you don't have a content calendar yet, follow these five steps and practice making one now.

#28
Optimizing Your Website

Creating your company website is a lengthy and personal process. Your website is a representation of who you are as a company, and therefore you want it to be the best representation possible. You also know how powerful an optimized website can be when planning out a digital marketing strategy. If search engine traffic is a primary way for your company to generate leads, your web pages must be effective.

Below are four search engine optimization techniques you can implement on your own to attract better quality leads. These changes may seem minor, but they will make the landing pages you already have in place more effective. Try these techniques and watch your online sales grow:

Go for quality, not quantity.

Having a lengthy page is important to prove credibility and boost search engine rankings, however long-form copy isn't always what site visitors want. If you keep your most important pages in the mid-range word count (350-500 words), while including photos and graphics to break up information segments, you're going to engage readers and keep them on your site longer. Long-form copy tends to have a higher bounce rate in certain cases, so it's important to add variety by giving your readers "the jist" in shorter articles and pages.

Think about titles, tags, and meta descriptions.

In the beginnings of SEO, tags and meta descriptions were at the forefront of optimization strategies. Since Google and other platforms have shifted to a focus on page content, so have many marketers. However, your titles, tags, and descriptions for pages are still essential to success. Titles and meta descriptions will attract better quality clicks, while tags help search engines correctly categorize your content. Spending a little more time on these areas will help you attract the kind of leads you want.

Optimize images.

Images are just as important to your content marketing as blog posts and pages, so including images on your web pages is obviously the first step. They break up content visually for the reader and make it easier to skim an article for important information. However, there are ways in which you can improve the quality of your images for even better results:

- Name the file using keywords related to the page
- Resize the image to fit better on the page
- Use your own images whenever possible
- If you must use stock photos, choose premium stock photos rather than free ones
- Make your own infographics and social media photos

Learn about link building.

The most important thing that search engines use to rank your content is backlinks. These are links from other websites that point back to your content, proving that your site and web page is "vetted" by other sites. The more closely related and more credible the site that links back to you is, the better your rankings will be. Rather than wait for people to link back to your content, you can reach out and collaborate with top-ranking industry sites to get them to link back to yours.
With these easy-to-implement strategies, you can take your content marketing strategy to the next level.

#29

6 Questions to Ask Before Hiring a Copywriter

Hiring a copywriter can change the game for your marketing initiatives. A professional writer can help you craft SEO-winning strategies for your site, create compelling press releases and brochures for your brand, and encourage you to do more with your marketing by handling all the time-consuming work. However, finding a quality writer that fits your company needs is not as easy as it sounds.

While there are thousands of writers available, few will provide the right pricing, quality, and consistency. Those with more experience will be able to promise better results, however they will come with higher rates. No matter what you want to do with your content marketing strategy, you need to find the right writer who can tackle the challenge and help your company grow.

Before you sign on the first copywriter you find, schedule an interview to learn more about their experience and services. To help you prepare, below are some questions you should ask the potential writer:

Why should I hire a freelance copywriter instead of a digital marketing firm or ad agency?

If you're looking to boost your content marketing results, you've likely thought about going through a digital marketing agency rather than hiring an individual contractor. While this may seem like the easy solution, you'll actually be spending much more for content you won't have much control over. Many ad agencies simply subcontract to a copywriter anyway, so you can cut out the middleman and hire your own directly that you know and trust.

Why should I hire you vs. another copywriter?

Asking this question directly will give the potential hire the opportunity to talk about their experience and specialties. Look for someone with:

- Client and agency references
- Experience in your field or in general business and marketing
- Someone who has been published on other platforms
- Published author or blog creator a plus

What services do you provide?

No two copywriters are alike, and many specialize in one industry or content medium. Some are pros at online content, while others write full-length books and biographies for influential people. You will also want to find out what other marketing services they provide, such as social media campaigning, consulting, PR work, or other areas you may need help.

What are your rates?

Copywriters all charge slightly differently. Some charge per project, while others offer package deals that include content for an entire content marketing campaign. You want someone who is affordable, but don't hire the cheapest and expect SEO-winning results. As with all business services, you get what you pay for. Always ask for a quote before signing a contract.

What are your terms?

Most copywriters are freelancers, and therefore create their own contract terms. While these may sometimes be negotiable, copywriters like to stay consistent with their clients not only to provide an equal service but to keep their own schedules manageable. Find out the exact terms of any contract with the copywriter before choosing them. Questions can include:

> When is payment due?
> When will I receive my copy?
> Who owns the copy once it is delivered? Do you require attribution?
> How do I pay you?
> How will I receive my finished copy?
> Do you offer preferred pricing/special terms for ongoing clients?

What happens if I don't like the first draft?

Even if you choose an excellent copywriter, sometimes your styles won't mesh, or you'll have a different vision for the piece than what is delivered. Discuss with your copywriter their policy on rewrites and editing. If you do receive a piece that you're not fully satisfied with, be vocal about what you like and don't like. It will help you both maintain a good relationship.

Asking these questions will help you create a strong working relationship with your copywriter before the first project begins.

Special Acknowledgements

Throughout my life, many have shared ideas, mentored and supported me. I wouldn't be where I am today without them. Although I may forget some, I'd like to thank Susan Greene, Amy Goodman, Jen Furda, and Sandi Vidal who have impacted my career with their advice, support, and friendship. They have each taught me valuable lessons in business, and today I can say I also value their friendship. There have been hundreds who have impacted my life for a season; knowing I'd forget many, I choose to leave them unnamed.

I have also been impacted by organizations that have taught me leadership and entrepreneurship that I've used in my business through the years. These organizations impacted me as a youth while participating in them and as an adult while volunteering with them. They are 4-H, DECA (Distributive Education Clubs of America), and Junior Achievement.

Most importantly are those closest to me. I have friends who have stood beside me through loss and triumph, adversity and victory, and have never wavered in their support. This list (and I hope I don't forget anyone!) includes Karen Johnson, Connie Justice, Scott Saunders, Kristi Grabill, Francis Lampasi, and I must mention Sandi Vidal and Amy Goodman once more.

I'd be remiss if I didn't mention my mom, brother, aunt, and grandma who influenced all my days with their unconditional love and support. And, the loves of my life, my children! I'd like to thank James and Tiffany for being my biggest cheerleaders and understanding the many hours I put into making my business grow. They love me, support me, offer their opinions, and give me the space to put in long hours. Thank you for all you mean to me!!

About Royce Gomez

Royce Gomez, founder of RoyceTalks, has been recognized as a leading authority for coaching and training entrepreneurs, which has included Ashoka sponsored events at Rollins College, Clinton Global Initiative University changemakers, Startup Weekend participants, business incubators and accelerators, venture pitch competitions, and SBDC events. Her articles have been published in the HuffingtonPost, Carol Roth, and other print and online media platforms. She has effectively coached successful business owners and written content for hundreds of companies. Royce's strategies increase revenue and her content gets results.

Royce started out modeling and in the fashion world before retail management then owning her own business. Since starting her first business, Royce has owned 12 different businesses. As a business coach, she has succeeded in a local storefront business, real estate investing, equine programs, image consulting, and home based businesses. She is a coach who works with business owners, not coaches. Because of extensive background in marketing, Royce has had the opportunity to write copy for Calvin Klein, DoubleTree, Keller Williams, Acti-Labs, Gone to Green and hundreds more.

Royce is the mother of 2 amazing adult children. She is an avid traveler and loves adventure, wine tasting, and music. Recently, she added kayaking as one of her favorite activities.

www.RoyceTalks.com   www.CoachingWithRoyce.com

Royce Gomez

www.ingramcontent.com/pod-product-compliance
Lightning Source LLC
Chambersburg PA
CBHW070643220526
45466CB00001B/269